CAMBRIDGE
Lower Secondary English

Lucy Birchenough, Julia Burchell, Clare Constant, Mike Gould, Naomi Hursthouse, Ian Kirby, Emma Page and Richard Vardy

Series Editors: Julia Burchell and Mike Gould

Stage 8: Student's Book

William Collins' dream of knowledge for all began with the publication of his first book in 1819. A self-educated mill worker, he not only enriched millions of lives, but also founded a flourishing publishing house. Today, staying true to this spirit, Collins books are packed with inspiration, innovation and practical expertise. They place you at the centre of a world of possibility and give you exactly what you need to explore it.

Collins. Freedom to teach.

Published by Collins
An imprint of HarperCollins*Publishers*
The News Building
1 London Bridge Street
London SE1 9GF

HarperCollins Publishers
1st Floor Watermarque Building
Ringsend Road Dublin 4 Ireland

Browse the complete Collins catalogue at
www.collins.co.uk

10 9 8 7 6 5

ISBN 978-0-00-836407-6

British Library Cataloguing-in-Publication Data
A catalogue record for this publication is available from the British Library.

Third-party websites, publications, publications and resources referred to in this publication have not been endorsed by Cambridge Assessment International Education.

We would like to thank the following teachers for their help in reviewing resources before publication: Abhinandan Bhattacharya, JBCN International School Oshiwara, Mumbai, India; Preeti Roychoudhury, Calcutta International School, Calcutta, India; Priya Saxena, Manthan International School, Hyderabad, India; Judith Hughes, International School of Budapest, Budapest, Hungary.

Series editor: Julia Burchell and Mike Gould
Authors: Lucy Birchenough, Julia Burchell, Clare Constant, Mike Gould, Naomi Hursthouse, Ian Kirby, Emma Page and Richard Vardy
Publisher: Elaine Higgleton
Product manager: Catherine Martin
Development editor: Judith Walters
Copyeditor: Catherine Dakin
Proofreader: Sonya Newland
Cover designer: Gordon McGilp
Cover illustration: Ann Paganuzzi
Typesetter: 2Hoots Publishing Services Ltd.
Production controller: Lyndsey Rogers
Printed and bound by Grafica Veneta S.p.A., Italy

Contents

Introduction   **5**

Chapter 1 Describing: Memorable characters   7

1.1 Enjoy reading   8
1.2 How characters are created: implicit and explicit meaning   12
1.3 Tracing character development   16
1.4 Exploring how writers use techniques to describe characters   20
1.5 Creating convincing characters   24
1.6 Creating rounded characters   28
1.7 Using punctuation for effect   32
1.8 Writing your own character description   34
1.9 Responding to a descriptive text   36

Chapter 2 Explaining: Great inventions   41

2.1 Enjoy reading   42
2.2 What is writing to explain?   44
2.3 Exploring how explanations are structured   48
2.4 Using formal and informal language in explanation texts   50
2.5 Collating and summarising information from two texts   52
2.6 Explaining things clearly in speech and presentations   54
2.7 Planning a report   58
2.8 Using connectives to explain clearly   60
2.9 Varying sentence structure to make explanations clear and engaging   62
2.10 Using colons and semicolons to include more detail   66
2.11 Writing your own explanatory article   68
2.12 Responding to a pair of explanation texts   72

Chapter 3 Arguing and persuading: Extreme sports   77

3.1 Enjoy reading   78
3.2 What is writing to argue and persuade?   82
3.3 Exploring how persuasive and argument texts are organised   86
3.4 Identifying main ideas and viewpoints   90
3.5 Reviewing persuasive techniques   94
3.6 Preparing a formal debate   96
3.7 Using phrases to develop persuasive sentences   100
3.8 Structuring an effective persuasive text   104
3.9 Writing your own persuasive letter   108
3.10 Responding to an argument text   112

Chapter 4 Narrating: A child's eye view — 117

4.1 Enjoy reading — 118
4.2 Exploring narrative perspective — 120
4.3 Exploring how writers create children's voices and viewpoints — 122
4.4 Investigating character with hot-seating — 126
4.5 Exploring alternative forms and structures for stories — 130
4.6 Developing a character's voice and viewpoint — 134
4.7 Using punctuation to develop character — 136
4.8 Structuring your own viewpoint narrative — 138
4.9 Writing a key moment from a child's viewpoint — 140
4.10 Responding to a narrative text — 144

Chapter 5 Exploring and discussing: Plays about conflict — 149

5.1 Enjoy reading — 150
5.2 Identifying key themes in a play — 152
5.3 Exploring themes through contrasting characters — 154
5.4 Developing your drama and discussion skills — 158
5.5 Structuring a response to themes in drama — 162
5.6 Responding to a playscript about conflict — 166

Chapter 6 Commenting and comparing: Poems and texts about growing up — 171

6.1 Enjoy reading — 172
6.2 Tracing how a narrator's views develop — 174
6.3 Commenting on how poets present childhood memories — 178
6.4 Comparing poems on a similar topic — 182
6.5 Sharing childhood experiences — 186
6.6 Writing your own poem about childhood — 188
6.7 Responding to two poems on the same theme — 190

Chapter 7 Testing your skills — 195

7.1 Reading and writing questions on non-fiction texts — 196
7.2 Reading and writing questions on fiction texts — 200
7.3 Assessing your progress: Reading and writing non-fiction — 204
7.4 Assessing your progress: Reading and writing fiction — 212

Glossary of key terms — 218

Acknowledgements — 220

Introduction

The Collins Stage 8 Student's Book offers a skills-building approach to the Cambridge Lower Secondary English curriculum framework.

The book is divided into seven chapters.

Chapters 1 to 6 each focus on a different writing 'purpose' or pair of writing purposes. For Stage 8, the chosen chapter focuses are describing, explaining, arguing and persuading, narrating, exploring and discussing, and commenting and comparing.

Each of these six chapters is based on a theme, such as 'poems about growing up' or 'great inventions' and enables you to develop and practise a range of reading, writing, speaking and listening skills within an engaging context. Skills are modelled clearly throughout to give you a method to follow and to show you how to progress.

You will read a rich range of international texts from different societies, cultures and eras, written in different forms and genres. These texts increase in length and challenge across Stage 8. You will also write a wide variety of texts yourself, learning from the texts and writers you are reading.

Each chapter provides you with opportunities to complete one or two substantial final tasks to apply your learning: one set of final reading tasks responding to a longer text, and in Chapters 1 to 4 one longer writing task. You will be able to assess your work against the sample responses provided to see how your abilities are developing.

Chapter 7 offers you the chance to put into practice the skills you have developed in Chapters 1 to 6, by responding to tasks on a non-fiction and a fiction text. You can then assess your work using the sample answers and guidance provided, to gain an understanding of where you might have gone wrong and how to improve your work.

The questions, example answers, suggested marks and/or comments that appear in this chapter are meant to be helpful advice for students and have been written by the authors of the textbook.

We hope our skills-building approach helps you and your teachers to fulfil the demands of your English course in an enjoyable and enriching way.

Julia Burchell and **Mike Gould**, Series Editors

Key features of the Student's Book

The opening page of each chapter summarises what you know and are already able to do from Stage 7 and what you will learn and produce in the chapter that follows.

A longer text is the focus of the first 'Enjoy reading' unit of each chapter.

Questions encourage you to share your first impressions of and personal responses to the text.

Vocabulary boxes support you to understand the extract.

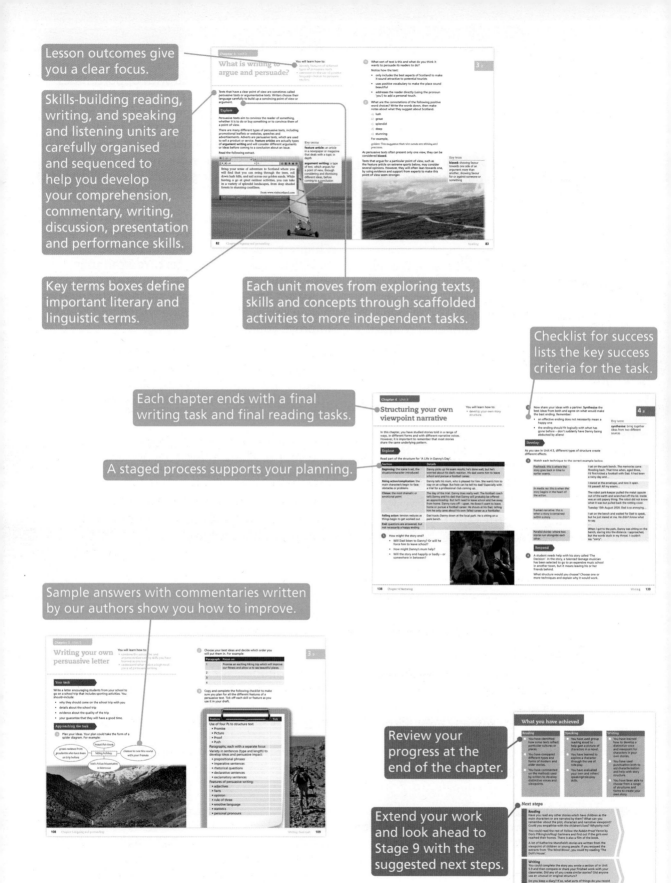

Lesson outcomes give you a clear focus.

Skills-building reading, writing, and speaking and listening units are carefully organised and sequenced to help you develop your comprehension, commentary, writing, discussion, presentation and performance skills.

Key terms boxes define important literary and linguistic terms.

Each unit moves from exploring texts, skills and concepts through scaffolded activities to more independent tasks.

Checklist for success lists the key success criteria for the task.

Each chapter ends with a final writing task and final reading tasks.

A staged process supports your planning.

Sample answers with commentaries written by our authors show you how to improve.

Review your progress at the end of the chapter.

Extend your work and look ahead to Stage 9 with the suggested next steps.

Chapter 1 Describing
Memorable characters

What's it all about?

This chapter is all about descriptive writing. You will focus on how writers describe real people and fictional characters convincingly. You will learn to show what characters are like and how they are feeling by choosing words carefully and by varying sentence length and style.

You should already know:
- that writers make choices to create effects
- how to describe places using effective details
- how to select words and sentence types to create atmosphere.

You will learn how to:
- identify and discuss explicit and implicit information about characters
- identify and discuss the structural features with which writers build and develop characters
- demonstrate understanding of speech, gesture and movement when creating and interpreting characters
- discuss in speech and writing how writers make characters complex and convincing
- select words and sentence types to create memorable and effective character descriptions in your own writing.

You will:
- explore how people are described in both fiction and non-fiction texts
- comment on the techniques writers use to create memorable characters
- adapt speech, gesture and movement to develop convincing characters
- select words and sentence types to create impact in a written character description.

Enjoy reading

You will learn how to:
- consider how readers build their impressions of characters
- respond to a descriptive text with understanding and insight.

You are going to read an extract from a novel called *Noah Barleywater Runs Away* by the Irish author John Boyne.

1 Think about the title of the novel.

a) What does the title make you think about?

b) What is barleywater and what does this name suggest about the main character?

c) Have you ever heard of John Boyne or anything else he has written?

d) What are you expecting the extract to be about?

2 Now read the extract slowly, noting down any words you are not sure about.

Vocabulary

barleywater: a sweet drink made from barley, sometimes flavoured with orange or lemon

Noah opened his eyes. It no longer felt as if all the puppets were crowding in on him, preparing to bury him beneath the weight of their bodies. The muttering had gone. The whispers had vanished. Instead they all seemed to have returned to their rightful places on 5 the shelves, and he realized how ridiculous it was even to have thought they were watching him or talking about him. They weren't real, after all; they were only puppets. But what *was* real was the elderly man who had spoken to him and who was now standing only 10 a few feet away, smiling a little, as if he had been expecting this visit for a very long time and was pleased that it had finally come to pass. He was holding a small block of wood in his hands and was chipping away at it with a small chisel as he stood there. Noah 15 swallowed quickly out of nervousness and, without meaning to, let out a sudden cry of surprise.

'Oh dear,' said the man, looking up from his work. 'There's no need for that, surely.'

'But there was no one here a moment ago,' said Noah, 20 looking around in astonishment. The door through which he had entered the shop was still nowhere to be seen, so where this man had appeared from was a mystery to him. 'And I didn't hear you come in.'

'I didn't mean to startle you,' said the man, who 25 was very old, even older than Noah's grandfather, with a mop of yellow hair that looked like porridge mixed with maize. He had very bright eyes that Noah found himself staring into, but the skin on his face was as wrinkled as any the boy had ever seen. 'I was 30 downstairs, working, that's all. And then I heard footsteps. So I thought I'd better come up and see whether a customer needed my attention.'

'I heard footsteps too,' said Noah. 'But I'm sure they were your footsteps, climbing the stairs.' 35

'Oh dear me, no,' said the old man, shaking his head. 'I could hardly have heard my own footsteps, then come up to investigate, could I? They must have been *your* footsteps.'

'But you were downstairs. You said as much.' 40

'Did I?' asked the old man, frowning and stroking his chin as he thought about it. 'I don't remember. It's all

so long ago now, isn't it? And I'm afraid my memory isn't what it once was. Perhaps I heard the bell over the door ring.' 45

'But there was no bell,' said Noah, and at that precise moment, as if it had just remembered its job, a cheerful ping sounded from above the door, which had now reappeared a few feet behind him.

'It's old too,' explained the old man with an apologetic 50 shrug. 'You wouldn't mind if it wasn't the only thing it had to do all day, but it forgets sometimes. That might not even have been you it was ringing for. It could be for a customer from last year.'

Noah turned round, open-mouthed, and stared at the 55 bell in surprise before turning back and swallowing loudly, unsure what he could possibly say to make sense of what had just taken place.

'Anyway, I'm sorry I kept you waiting for so long,' said the old man, 'but I'm afraid I move like a snail these 60 days. It's not like it was when I was a young man. You wouldn't have seen me for dust back them.'

From *Noah Barleywater Runs Away* by John Boyne

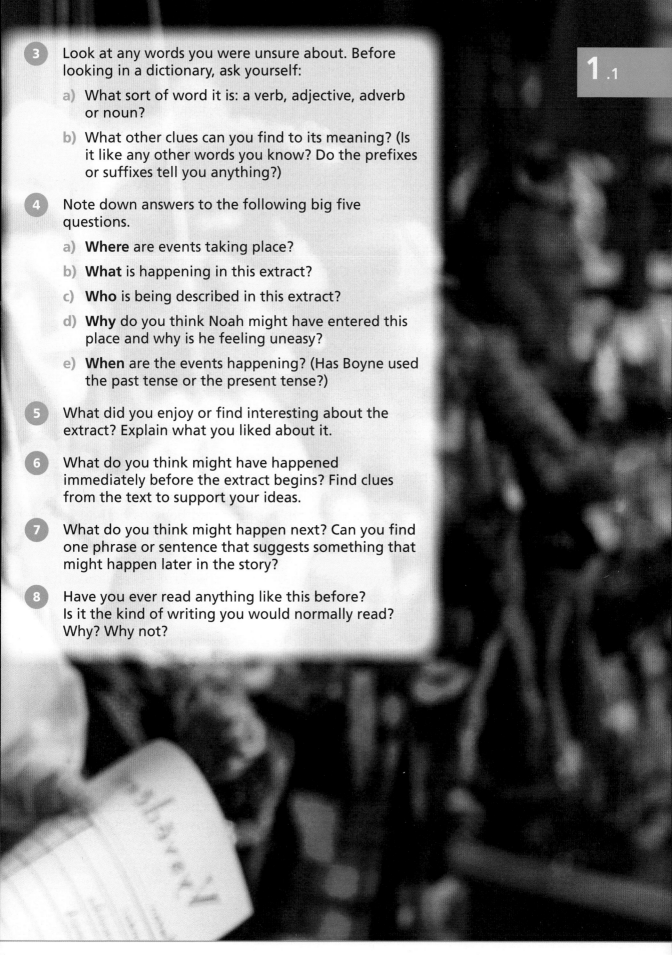

3 Look at any words you were unsure about. Before looking in a dictionary, ask yourself:

 a) What sort of word it is: a verb, adjective, adverb or noun?

 b) What other clues can you find to its meaning? (Is it like any other words you know? Do the prefixes or suffixes tell you anything?)

4 Note down answers to the following big five questions.

 a) **Where** are events taking place?

 b) **What** is happening in this extract?

 c) **Who** is being described in this extract?

 d) **Why** do you think Noah might have entered this place and why is he feeling uneasy?

 e) **When** are the events happening? (Has Boyne used the past tense or the present tense?)

5 What did you enjoy or find interesting about the extract? Explain what you liked about it.

6 What do you think might have happened immediately before the extract begins? Find clues from the text to support your ideas.

7 What do you think might happen next? Can you find one phrase or sentence that suggests something that might happen later in the story?

8 Have you ever read anything like this before? Is it the kind of writing you would normally read? Why? Why not?

How characters are created: implicit and explicit meaning

You will learn how to:
- locate relevant explicit information in a text
- infer additional information about characters from the writer's choice of language.

When a writer describes a person – whether it is a real person or an imaginary one – they usually combine direct information with more subtle clues about them. In this way, readers build an overall impression of the person in their minds.

Vocabulary

lustre: glow

testified: was evidence of

hawser: thick rope

steed: horse

stirrups: supports for feet

Explore

 1 Read the two descriptive extracts below. For each extract, say *who* is being described.

Extract A

A little old man descended after them into the boat; presently his horse was also let down by means of a crane. This was the officer in command. He was a middling-sized but very muscular old fellow, already beyond his seventieth and not very far from his eightieth year; but he was as vigorous now both in mind and body as he had been when his beard, which now swept across his breast like the wing of a swan, was as dark as the raven's plume.

His broad shoulders spoke of extraordinary strength, while the firm expression of his face, the flashing **lustre** of his eyes, and his calm and valiant look, **testified** to the fact that this strength was squandered upon no coward soul.

Some stout rowing brought the boat at last near to the shore, but not all the efforts of the men could bring her to land; the wash of the sea was so great that the foam-crested waves again and again drove the boat back from the shore.

At a sign from the old man three of the ship's crew leaped into the waves in order to drag after them the boat's **hawser**, but the sea tore it out of the hands of all three as easily as a wild bull would toss a pack of children.

Then the old man vaulted upon his **steed**, kicking the **stirrups** aside, and leaped among the churning waves. Twice the horse was jostled back by the assault of the foaming billows, but at the third attempt the shore was reached. The people on the shore said it was a miracle; but he, wasting no words upon any one, directed his way all alone along the shore of the haven.

From *The Lion of Janina* by Mór Jókai, translated by R. Nisbet Bain

Extract B

Benedict Allen arrives dressed like an explorer: all in green, multi-pocketed jacket, sturdy trousers, a bag that could carry accessories in the Amazon. It is a somewhat **anachronistic** get-up for a meeting in central London, at **the Savoy hotel**, but very useful given that we want a picture of him in the gardens next to **the Embankment**, which, for our purposes, will double as a jungle.

He takes the artifice like a trooper, pushing aside the ferns as if he was yomping to a lost city in Amazonia, but proves less adept once we are seated in the hotel, having difficulty making clear just how large a pot of tea he wants and turning away the nuts and olives because he doesn't realise they are complimentary. 'Sorry, I'm not your usual class of guest,' he says to the bemused waitress. After spending so much of his life in wildernesses, he admits he finds it difficult adapting to this more refined jungle, but it may also be a natural trait: tall, gangly and prone to gesticulating wildly to express himself, he was not made for sipping tea in hotel bars. He was made for a life of adventure.

From 'Meet Benedict Allen, the explorer rescued by the Daily Mail against his will' by Stephen Moss, *The Guardian*, 28 June 2018

Vocabulary

anachronistic: belonging to another period in history

the Savoy Hotel: a luxurious hotel in central London famous for its afternoon tea

the Embankment: an area next to the River Thames in London

2 For each extract, think about whether it is taken from a fiction or from a non-fiction text. Provide reasons to support your ideas.

> I think Extract A is taken from a fiction/non-fiction
> text because…
> I think Extract B is taken from a fiction/non-fiction
> text because…

3 **a)** Both writers provide readers with some **explicit information** about the person they are describing. For each of the following pieces of information, say whether it tells us something about the officer (O) or Benedict (B).

- He is tall.
- He is between 70 and 80 years old.
- His clothes are green.
- He carries a bag.
- He has a beard.
- He doesn't speak to the people on the shore.

b) Copy and complete the following table with explicit information you have retrieved from the text. You might not be able to fill in all the details.

	The old officer	Benedict Allen
What does he look like?		
What does he wear?		
What does he say?		
How does he move?		
What does he do?		

c) In pairs, summarise what you have learned about the two figures being described. What overall impression of each person do you think the writer is trying to convey?

> **Key term**
>
> **explicit information:** information that can be retrieved directly, without having to read between the lines

Develop

Sometimes information about a character is **implicit**. The writer provides clues so that readers can deduce and **infer** additional information about the character and build an overall impression.

Look at this annotation made about a quotation from Extract A:

'flashing lustre of his eyes'

4 Write your own annotation for the following quotation to explain what it suggests about the man's character and behaviour.

'wasting no words upon anyone'

5 Now copy and annotate the following quotation from Extract B.

'He takes the artifice like a trooper.'

6 Select a quotation from one of the two extracts that provides the reader with another insight about either the old officer or Benedict Allen. Copy it out and annotate it to show the effect of the words used.

Respond

7 Think of a person you admire and list the qualities you like in that person. Now write a paragraph about him or her. As well as including explicit details (such as their appearance), you should provide clues that will help your readers to infer additional information (such as their personal qualities).

Key terms

implicit: what is shown or suggested in a text (the writer does not provide this information directly but gives the reader clues)

infer: to work out what someone is implying through their choice of words

Suggests that he is full of life and energy, like a bright, gleaming light.

Tracing character development

You will learn how to:
- explore how character is revealed and developed throughout a text
- use relevant references to support your ideas.

Writers **imply** things about a character through descriptive language. They may also describe the same features in different ways throughout a piece of writing to show how the character changes and develops.

Explore

When a writer introduces a villain into their story, they may not reveal straight away how bad the character is. This makes it more exciting for the reader when they discover the villain's true nature.

1. Read the following extract and answer the big five questions.

   a) **What** is happening in this extract?

   b) **Who** is telling the story?

   c) **Where** is the extract set?

   d) **When** does Dracula make a move towards his visitor?

   e) **Why** might Jonathan be visiting Dracula?

2. Think about how the writer introduces the character. What impression do you get of Dracula? Does this change as you read on through the extract?

> **Key term**
>
> **imply:** to suggest something, through your choice of words, rather than saying it directly

Extract 1

> Within, stood a tall old man, clean shaven save for a long white moustache, and clad in black from head to foot, without a single speck of colour about him anywhere. The old man motioned me in with his right hand with a **courtly** gesture, saying in excellent English, but with a strange intonation: 'Welcome to my house! Enter freely and of your own will!' He made no motion of stepping to meet me, but stood like a statue, as though his gesture of welcome had fixed him into stone. The instant, however, that I had stepped over the threshold, he moved impulsively forward, and holding out his hand grasped mine with a strength which made me wince, an effect which was not lessened by the fact that it seemed as cold as ice—more like the hand of a dead than a living man.
>
> From *Dracula* by Bram Stoker

> **Vocabulary**
>
> **courtly:** very polite in an old-fashioned, formal and possibly regal way

3　Look at the following quotations from the extract. Which ones make Dracula seem polite and harmless and which ones make him seem strange and creepy?

a) 'a tall old man, clean shaven'

b) 'clad in black from head to foot, without a single speck of colour'

c) 'The old man motioned me in with his right hand with a courtly gesture'

d) '"Welcome to my house!"'

e) 'holding out his hand grasped mine with a strength which made me wince'

f) 'it seemed as cold as ice—more like the hand of a dead than a living man'

4　Using the quotations from Question 3, copy and complete the table below. An example has been given.

Highlight one detail from the quotation (a word, phrase or punctuation mark)	Identify the technique used here	What this detail suggests about Dracula
a) 'a tall old man, clean shaven'		
b) 'clad in black from head to foot, without a single speck of colour'		
c) 'The old man motioned me in with his right hand with a courtly gesture'	adjective	suggests he is being friendly and showing his visitor respect
d) '"Welcome to my house!"'		
e) 'holding out his hand grasped mine with a strength which made me wince'		
f) 'it seemed as cold as ice—more like the hand of a dead than a living man'		

Writers often focus on specific features of a character's appearance, such as their face, and leave readers to infer what their appearance suggests about that character. When exploring how a character develops, it can be a good idea to track how a particular feature is described, such as movement, facial features or expressions, clothing or speech.

Read the next extract from *Dracula*, looking closely for references to Dracula's facial features.

Extract 2

His face was a strong—a very strong—**aquiline**, with high bridge of the thin nose and peculiarly arched nostrils. His eyebrows were very massive, almost meeting over the nose, and with bushy hair that seemed to curl in its own profusion. The mouth, so far as I could see it under the heavy moustache, was fixed and rather cruel-looking, with peculiarly sharp white teeth; these protruded over the lips, whose remarkable **ruddiness** showed astonishing vitality in a man of his years. For the rest, his ears were pale, and at the tops extremely pointed; the chin was broad and strong, and the cheeks firm though thin. The general effect was one of extraordinary **pallor**.

From *Dracula* by Bram Stoker

Vocabulary

aquiline: curved

ruddiness: redness

pallor: pale appearance

5 Using details from the extract, make a sketch of Dracula's face. Label your sketch with quotations from the passage. For example, his eyebrows should be 'almost meeting' and 'bushy'.

6 Next, look at the labels on your sketch. What different impressions do these descriptions give you of Dracula? Add to your labels to explain what each facial feature suggests about him. For example:

> The adjective 'pale' and the noun 'pallor' show that Dracula has skin that is unusually white and bloodless. This could suggest that Dracula is someone who avoids daylight, or that he is ill or dying.

Develop

Read the following extract from later in the novel. Once again, the story is told in the first person from the perspective of a young Englishman called Jonathan Harker who has travelled overseas to visit Dracula on business.

The writer develops the **characterisation** of Dracula after he is angered by a group of women that live under his roof and are his servants.

Key term

characterisation: the way a character is created and developed by a writer

Extract 3

Never did I imagine such **wrath** and fury, [...]. His eyes were positively blazing. The red light in them was **lurid**, as if [...flames] blazed behind them. His face was deathly pale, and the lines of it were hard like drawn wires; the thick eyebrows that met over the nose now seemed like a heaving bar of white-hot metal. With a fierce sweep of his arm, he hurled the woman from him. In a voice which, though low and almost in a whisper seemed to cut through the air and then ring round the room he said: 'Back, I tell you all! This man belongs to me!'

From *Dracula* by Bram Stoker

Vocabulary
....

wrath: anger

lurid: unnaturally bright

7   Copy and complete the following table to compare how Dracula's physical appearance is presented across the three extracts.

	Quotations from Extracts 1 and 2 that make Dracula seem *harmless/welcoming*	Quotations from Extracts 1 and 2 that make Dracula seem *odd/creepy*	Quotations from Extract 3 that make Dracula seem *terrifying/violent*
skin/complexion		'The general effect was one of extraordinary pallor.'	
movements	'The old man motioned me in with his right hand with a courtly gesture.'		
eyes and eyebrows			'His eyes were positively blazing. The red light in them was lurid, as if [... flames] blazed behind them.'
voice			
nose and mouth			

Respond

8   Work with a partner. Each choose a different row from your completed table and explain to each other how Bram Stoker develops the character of Dracula to gradually reveal his true villainous nature.

For each quotation, pick out a particular word or technique Stoker uses to present Dracula in that way.

Exploring how writers use techniques to describe characters

You will learn how to:
- consider a range of techniques used to describe characters
- comment on the implications and effects of specific words and phrases.

Writers use descriptive language to imply things to the reader about characters, and to create different effects.

> **Explore**

Writers sometimes use descriptions of nature or the weather to reflect what a character is feeling. This technique is called **pathetic fallacy** and it can be useful in creating a particular atmosphere.

> **Key term**
>
> **pathetic fallacy:** using a description of the weather to reflect the feelings of a character

1 What types of weather might be linked to the following feelings? Give reasons for each of your choices.

a) happiness

b) sadness

c) anger

d) calmness

e) fear

Writers can also suggest ideas about character through the way their surroundings are described.

Read the extract below. It is set in India and describes an older woman, Baby Kochamma, and her servant.

Filth had laid siege to the Ayemenem house like a medieval army advancing on an enemy castle. It clotted every crevice and clung to the windowpanes.

Midges whizzed in teapots. Dead insects lay in empty vases.

The floor was sticky. White walls had turned an uneven grey. Brass hinges and doorhandles were dull and greasy to the touch. Infrequently used plug points were clogged with grime. Lightbulbs had a film of oil on them. The only things that shone were the giant cockroaches that scurried around like varnished

gofers on a film set.

Baby Kochamma had stopped noticing these things long ago. Kochu Maria, who noticed everything, had stopped caring.

The **chaise longue** on which Baby Kochamma reclined had crushed peanut shells stuffed into the crevices of its rotting upholstery.

In an unconscious gesture of television-enforced **democracy**, mistress and servant both scrabbled unseeingly in the same bowl of nuts. Kochu Maria tossed nuts into her mouth. Baby Kochamma *placed* them **decorously** in hers.

By Arundhati Roy

Vocabulary

gofer: a person who is sent off to do lots of little jobs

chaise longue: a type of sofa

democracy: equal treatment

decorously: in a careful and polite way

2 List all the references to the filth or neglect of the house that you can find in the extract.

3 What do these descriptions suggest about Baby Kochamma? Choose one of the following options and then note down the reasons for your choice.

a) They suggest Baby Kochamma is poor and can't afford to clean the house.

b) They suggest she likes the house being dirty.

c) They suggest she has given up and lives in the past not the present.

Develop

Where a writer has used pathetic fallacy or description of settings to convey character, being able to explain *how* this has been achieved is an important skill. To do this, you need to explore the range of choices and techniques that create the effect.

4 Look at the extract again.

a) Identify between three and five phrases that were the most memorable and helped you to imagine both the house and Baby Kochamma's character. Write each one on a separate piece of paper or index card.

b) Annotate each phrase to highlight the range of techniques used. For example, you could select the phrase 'Midges whizzed in tea-pots' and highlight the use of **onomatopoeia** in the word 'whizzed' .

Key term

onomatopoeia: when a word sounds like the thing it describes (e.g. 'whisper', 'crash')

Checklist for success

✔ word choices

✔ **imagery**

✔ sound effects

✔ the senses

✔ sentence length and structure

Key term
....
imagery: language intended
to conjure up a vivid picture
in the reader's mind

 a) Overall, which technique did you think was most effective? Justify your ideas.

b) Compare your choices and your ideas with two other students. How did you each reach your decisions about which techniques were the most effective? Argue the case for why your choice is the best.

> ## Respond

It is important that you explore the effect of a technique in depth. You can do this by carefully unpicking the different meanings of certain words and phrases, rather than writing in a general way.

 Look at the two examples below, written by students exploring the phrase 'Midges whizzed in teapots'. Which do you think is the most successful piece of writing – A or B? Why?

Response A

> The writer uses onomatopoeia in the text: 'Midges whizzed in tea-pots'. This describes the movement of the insects.

Response B

> The writer uses onomatopoeia to describe the movement and sound of the insects as they 'whizzed in teapots'. The use of the word 'whizzed' suggests their speedy circling and high-pitched buzzing. It adds to the idea of 'filth' invading.

The flow chart below shows you how to develop a response to a question.

> How does Arundhati Roy create a memorable picture of the house and how does she use it to portray Baby Kochamma?

Start by thinking about what the writer is trying to convey about the house (it is dirty and neglected).

Support this with a relevant textual reference.

Explore how the writer has made the house seem dirty and neglected. Identify which words have this effect. Explain which senses they appeal to. What techniques has Arundhati Roy used?

Link your commentary to the picture created of Baby Kochamma.

7 Write four or five points as a developed response to the following question:

How does Arundhati Roy create a memorable picture of the house and how does she use it to portray Baby Kochamma?

Checklist for success

✔ Select relevant textual references.

✔ Identify the most effective techniques used by the writer.

✔ Comment on the effects of specific words and phrases.

Creating convincing characters

You will learn how to:
- adapt the way you talk, gesture and move to create different effects
- comment on effects created and techniques used.

Speakers and performers can vary their speech, gestures and movement in many ways. These techniques help audiences to understand and **empathise** with what characters are thinking and feeling.

Key term

empathise: understand the feelings of others

Explore

1. In pairs, read aloud this short script.

   A: Hello. Is anyone home?

   B: Sorry. I was upstairs. Can I help you?

   A: The door was open so I let myself in. I've come to collect a parcel.

   B: A parcel? I think you might have the wrong address. Let me see that…

   A: This is definitely the right house. I was here last week. Don't you remember?

2 **a)** Each speaker should select a different **stage direction** from the grid. Think about how to adapt your voice, gestures and movements to convey this stage direction. Then reread the script aloud making these adaptations. Can your partner work out which stage direction you chose? Repeat this activity a few different ways, varying the stage directions used.

suspicious	relaxed	tired
lying	defensive	wanting to help
confused	angry	seeing the funny side
meaning the other person harm	curious	distracted
nervous	desperate to share a secret	in awe of the other person
irritated	embarrassed	businesslike

b) Next, imagine that the visitor (Speaker B) is one of the following: a police officer; a head teacher; a local politician or community leader. Keeping the overall meaning the same, redraft the short script using formal **standard English**, such as a more formal greeting; no contractions; full sentences, more formal vocabulary. Then read the script aloud and reflect on the impact of your language choices.

3 Decide which version of the script you thought was the most convincing. In your pair, rehearse your final version to perform in front of the class. Memorising your lines will help you make good use of gestures and movements in your performance.

4 Now take it in turns to perform the script to the class. After each performance, reflect on what you have seen and heard using the prompts below.

a) What could you infer about Speaker A from their voice, gestures and movements?

b) What could you infer about Speaker B from their voice, gesture and movements?

Key terms

stage direction: an instruction within a playscript describing how the text should be performed

standard English: the most widely used form of English which is not specific to a particular place or region

5   **a)** The following three short extracts all come from plays by William Shakespeare. Each extract has two speaking parts. Based *only* on the evidence of the five lines of script you are given (A, B or C) decide what you think might be going on in this extract. Which words and phrases helped you to infer this?

   b) Using the stage direction cards from Question 2a), try out different ways of speaking, gesturing and moving. Think about the different effects you can create, which version you prefer and why.

Extract A

ANNE:	I would I knew thy heart.
GLOUCESTER:	'Tis figured in my tongue.
ANNE:	I fear me both are false.
GLOUCESTER:	Then never was man true.
ANNE:	Well, well, put up your sword.

From *Richard III* by William Shakespeare

Extract B

MACBETH:	How now! What news?
LADY MACBETH:	He has almost supped. Why have you left the chamber?
MACBETH:	Hath he asked for me?
LADY MACBETH:	Know you not, he has?
MACBETH:	We will proceed no further in this business:

From *Macbeth* by William Shakespeare

Extract C

BENEDICK:	Lady Beatrice, have you wept all this while?
BEATRICE:	Yea, and I will weep a while longer.
BENEDICK:	I will not desire that.
BEATRICE:	You have no reason. I do it freely.
BENEDICK:	Surely I do believe your fair cousin is wronged.

From *Much Ado About Nothing* by William Shakespeare

You might like to annotate your script to remind you of some of your best ideas about developing convincing characters on stage.

Respond

6 **a)** Take it in turns to perform one of your Shakespeare scenes for the class.

b) After each scene, the rest of the class should share their impressions of the two characters in terms of

- the characters' situation
- their thoughts and feelings
- their motivation within the scene.

They should explain how they reached their conclusions.

c) Discuss this feedback with your partner and evaluate how effectively you communicated your intended ideas about your characters.

Creating rounded characters

You will learn how to:

- write detailed descriptions to show different aspects of a character
- use varied vocabulary to engage the reader and sustain interest.

When writing at length about a character or person in a piece of descriptive writing, it is a good idea to write in detail about a number of different aspects of your character.

Explore

1 Read the following two sentences. Consider how much or how little we learn about the characters mentioned in them, and what it is that we learn about them.

> The man crossed the road.

> The dark-haired woman got into the car.

Using the different senses will help the reader imagine the characters you are describing in more detail. You can use:

- sight: colours, shapes
- touch: textures, temperatures
- smell/taste: perfume or workplace odours, for example
- sound: tone of voice or someone's laugh, for example.

2 Add one descriptive detail to each of the sentences in Question 1.

3 Write a list of words you could use to describe someone's physical build, and another list of words you could use to describe someone's hair – see the examples below. Use as many of the senses as you can and some hyphenated **compound words**, for example, sweet-smelling, honey-coloured.

Build	Hair
skinny	tangled
big-boned	soft
short	side-parted

Key term

compound word: two words joined together to form a new word

4 Some of the words you listed for the previous question might have had similar meanings but different connotations and implications. For example, the words 'slim', 'svelte', 'scrawny' and 'skinny' are all synonyms for 'thin' but have different connotations.

a) Create a word wheel with the word 'thin' at its centre and then write synonyms for 'thin' on the wheel's spokes. Add notes about the implications of each word and whether each word has positive (+), negative (-) or neutral connotations.

b) Create word wheels for some more adjectives, such as 'short', 'soft', 'big', 'long', 'tall', 'curly', and repeat the exercise to analyse their connotations.

Develop

Read this description:

> Her unruly, scarlet hair flashed like fire as she pelted down the road, her feet pounding the pavement with urgency.

5 a) Pick out two specific adjectives the writer has used and note down their effects.

b) Pick out three powerful verbs the writer has used and note down their effects.

c) Identify any further language techniques the writer has used and their effects.

d) Write a few sentences explaining how the writer has conveyed character effectively in this short description.

Now read the following two descriptions of a man's hands.

> Stretched tightly over the knuckles, his light brown skin was rough like old leaves ready to crumble into dust.

> His brown hands looked old.

6 The first description is more detailed and imaginative.

a) Which language techniques have been used and why are they effective?

b) As well as sight, which senses have been used to convey character?

c) Write a sentence about your own hands. Aim to choose words that not only describe the appearance of your hands but provide a deeper impression of you as a person.

Choosing a range of details is important when you are writing at length. It can be helpful at the planning stage to identify different aspects of your person or character and then to focus on each of these details in turn as you write.

7 How might someone describe you if they saw you today? Create a spider diagram that records different features of your appearance that someone observant might notice, such as the length of your fingernails, the type of footwear, the colour of your eyes and your expression or posture. Challenge yourself to think of precise words and images to convey the particular effect you are aiming for.

8 Look back at your answer to Question 7. Choose one of the features of your own appearance and write a short paragraph describing this feature in detail.

Checklist for success

✔ Choose precise words and consider their connotations.

✔ Try to appeal other senses as well as the sense of sight.

✔ Use a range of language and literary techniques, e.g. sound effects and imagery.

Read the following short descriptions.

A

The warm sand as he strolled felt as soft as silk beneath his blistered feet.

B

She read the local newspaper every day without fail, carefully scanning every page. Her brow would furrow as she searched line by line for news of him.

C

I was breathing so deeply by then I thought my heart would escape from my chest. Summoning all my strength, I hurled the ball into the air and swung my racket overhead like a **trebuchet**. Ball and racket met in mid-air with a loud 'thwack!'

Vocabulary

trebuchet: a large catapult once used in siege warfare, with a swinging wooden arm to launch projectiles

9 a) Identify the techniques that are being using to convey character. Copy and annotate each description to show the techniques used and what can be inferred about the character.

b) The writers of these examples have remembered a useful piece of advice: 'show, don't tell'. What do you think each writer is trying to show or suggest to us about the main character?

- Where is the character?

- What are they doing?

- How do they feel?

- What do they need or want?

c) Which words and phrases provide these clues about characters? Add these ideas to your annotations.

10 Write a story opening that introduces a key character using 'show, don't tell'.

Checklist for success

✔ Use precise verbs to show what is happening.

✔ Show how a character is feeling through your description of their actions.

✔ Use the senses to help the reader imagine they are experiencing events for themselves.

Using punctuation for effect

You will learn how to:
- use colons and parenthetical commas accurately
- use punctuation to develop and deepen characterisation.

As you become more confident in your descriptive writing, you should start to use a wider range of punctuation. This will make your sentences more interesting to read, and help you to build up your ideas and make your characters more complex and believable.

Explore

Commas and dashes can be used parenthetically (like brackets) to add extra detail in the middle of sentences. The information to the left of the first comma and the right of your second comma should make sense when joined together. For example:

> The box of pencils, a gift from her grandmother, was the first item she packed in her suitcase.

> The opera singer – wearing a beautiful red ballgown and with a rose in her hair – captivated the audience with her performance.

1. How does the information added using commas or dashes help the reader to understand character and motivation in each of the sentences above?

2. Add parenthetical commas to the following sentences.

   a) She ran her heart beating with panic towards the exit.

   b) The old man stretching his exhausted limbs opened his eyes.

   c) Leo still ashamed of the way he had spoken to his coach last week picked up his sports bag and headed to the training session.

Colons introduce a list or emphasise an idea. A colon can be used to create a dramatic pause before important information. The information that comes before the colon must make sense on its own. For example:

> He remembered his mother in easier, happier times: her love of treats and parties, her stylish appearance, her musical laughter.

> She watched him, so smart in his uniform, as he entered the building: his first day at school had begun.

3 In each of the examples above, what might the pause created by the colon represent?

4 Copy out the following sentences, putting colons in the correct places.

a) He put his head in his hands and thought of all the things he'd lost home, family, friends, self-respect.

b) Spinning the steering wheel and accelerating, Amit sped around the street corner and on towards the hotel only five minutes remained.

c) She looked up at the clouds with gratitude sunlight beamed down at last.

Respond

5 Write a descriptive paragraph that conveys a character's thoughts, feelings and motivations as well as their actions. You could use one of the sentences from Question 4 as your opening sentence. Include:

a) two sentences that use parenthetical commas/ dashes

b) one sentence that uses a colon

c) another type of punctuation to help the reader understand the character's thinking, such as a question mark or ellipsis.

Writing your own character description

You will learn how to:
- combine the descriptive writing skills you have learned
- understand what makes good descriptive writing.

Your task

Invent and describe a character who is a superhero.

Approaching the task

1. Create a mind map or use another planning format to focus your thoughts about your superhero.

2. Decide the sequence in which you will present your ideas. For example:

   a) flying – describe costume and speed of flight

   b) landing in a street – describe facial appearance and body language

   c) saving someone's life – describe movements, strength and speech

3. Think about the techniques you will use to describe your superhero:

   - adjectives
   - descriptive verbs
   - listing of details
   - repetition
   - imagery
   - appeal to the senses
   - short sentences
   - varied punctuation.

4. Come up with an engaging opening sentence that describes the superhero in action in a way that also shows us something about their appearance, abilities or character. For example:

   > Like a speeding train, a muscular, scarlet-clad figure swooped through the clouds.

5. Now write your description. When you have finished, check through your work for any errors in spelling, punctuation and grammar.

Reflecting on your work

6 Compare your own response to Question 5 with the two responses below. Using the comments, identify ways in which your own response could be improved and rewrite it, if needed.

Response 1

Ice Girl stepped from the lake. Her skin was blue and covered in delicate frost. Her white nails were like icicles and her hair was full of snowflakes. Her white robes shimmered in the sunlight and icy footprints formed as she walked across the grass.

> Opening sentence introduces the character but could contain a bit more description.

> Interesting description of her skin, but could be more precise about the shade of 'blue'.

> Imaginative simile.

> Interesting description but could be developed further to help the reader visualise this.

> Good descriptive details but a greater range of techniques could be used.

Comment on Response 1

This is a good start, although the description of features could be more fully developed. There are some good uses of vocabulary and descriptive techniques, but the choice of adjectives could be more imaginative. There could be more variety in the sentence types and sentence openers used.

Response 2

The frozen lake cracked open and Ice Girl emerged from the cold, dark waters. Cool blue and glistening like marble, her skin was covered in delicate frost. Her sharp nails, droplets of water falling from the glacial tips, were like icicles. As she moved, tiny snowflakes floated from her white, wintry hair like a silvery cloud all around her.

    Her glassy robes shimmering in the sunlight, she glided towards the bank of the lake. Landing barefoot on the grass, she left glittery, icy footprints where she stepped.

> Plenty of powerful and precise verbs.

> Some interesting similes but the description would benefit from a greater variety of techniques.

> Well-chosen adjectives help to develop descriptions.

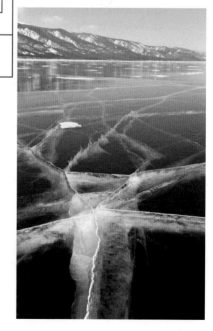

Comment on Response 2

The student has used interesting verbs and adjectives, and the descriptions help the reader visualise different details. The writing would benefit from a wider variety of imagery, such as metaphor. Complex sentences are effectively used to add information and build an overall impression of the character.

Responding to a descriptive text

You will learn how to:

- write a commentary on descriptive techniques and their effects
- evaluate your own commentary writing and work to improve it.

You are going to explore the ways in which John Boyne presents the toymaker using the understanding you have built up throughout this chapter.

Understanding the text

Look again at the extract on pages 9 to 10.

1 Write a sentence in response to each of these questions.

   a) The extract presents us with an encounter with the toymaker from Noah's point of view. Find two quotations that provide the reader with clues about Noah (his personality, appearance, feelings, experiences).

   b) How would you describe Noah's first impressions of the toymaker in this extract? Provide evidence to support your view.

Thinking about the text's purpose and features

2 Look again at the extract. Why does Boyne choose to go into detail in describing the toymaker? Complete the grid with quotations and relevant line numbers.

Feature	Quotation(s) and line number(s)
physical build and features	
speech and voice	
gestures and movements	
how he treats others	
how others behave around him	
background/backstory	

Looking at the text in detail

3 The writer has presented the character of the toymaker using a range of techniques.

Reread these sentences from the extract and answer the questions.

a) 'He had very bright eyes that Noah found himself staring into, but the skin on his face was as wrinkled as any the boy had ever seen.' (lines 27–30)

Find two adjectives in this sentence and explain what they imply about the toymaker.

b) '"Did I?" asked the old man, frowning and stroking his chin as he thought about it.' (lines 41–42)

Pick out the two verbs in this sentence that show the toymaker's movements and gestures. What might we infer from these choices?

c) The door through which he had entered the shop was still nowhere to be seen, so where this man had appeared from was a mystery to him. (lines 21–24)

  i. What do you think Boyne might be implying about the toymaker here?

  ii. Find three more words and phrases from the text that also help to create this impression of the toymaker.

d) 'with a mop of yellow hair that looked like porridge mixed with maize' (lines 27–28)

Identify the **metaphor** and **simile** in this description, and comment on their effect in describing the toymaker's appearance.

e) Copy out an example of each of the following:
(i) a sentence where an additional detail has been included between parenthetical commas;
(ii) a sentence with a semicolon; (iii) a short simple sentence. Explain the effect of at least one of these sentence level choices.

f) Select two things that the toymaker says. How do these quotations contribute to our impressions of the toymaker? (Think about the toymaker's style of speaking as well as the content of what he is saying.)

g) Highlight and count up all the references in the passage to the toymaker's age. Then pick two or three of these words and phrases and consider how they contribute to our overall impression of the toymaker.

Key terms
....

metaphor: a type of comparison that describes one thing as if it is something else (e.g. 'Our garden is a jungle')

simile: a comparison between two things that uses the words 'as' or 'like' (e.g. 'Our garden is like a jungle')

4 Write three paragraphs commenting on your first impressions of the toymaker and the techniques Boyne has used to create this impression.

You could use these sentence starters:

The toymaker seems…

This is shown by…

The word/phrase/sentence '…' suggests…

The detail between parenthetical commas emphasises…

Reflecting on your work

5 Compare your own response to Question 4 to the two below. Once you have read them, identify ways in which your own response could be improved. Rewrite it, if needed.

Response 1

The toymaker is presented as an old man. This is shown by the repeated use of the word 'old' and by other words such as 'elderly' and 'wrinkled'. He is also shown to be rather mysterious. Boyne writes that 'where this man had appeared from was a mystery to him'. This suggests that even though the man seems to be very elderly and sometimes forgetful or confused, he might have some kind of special powers.

- An accurate impression noted.
- Simple evidence in the form of key words used, given to support point.
- A second accurate impression noted.
- Supportive evidence given in the form of a short quotation.
- An overview of the two impressions is given, which adds an impression drawn from an inference.

Comment on Response 1

This directly answers the question and makes two clear points about how the toymaker is described. Both points are supported by textual evidence. The answer explores the toymaker's appearance as well as clues about his character. To improve on this answer, the interesting point about 'special powers' could be explored in more depth, and more key terms could be used.

Response 2

The toymaker is an intriguing character from the beginning of the extract onwards. In the first paragraph, Boyne describes him smiling 'as if he had been expecting this visit for a very long time'. This suggests that the toymaker might have some kind of powers of prediction. His appearance also makes a strong impression on Noah; his advanced age is emphasised when the author stresses between parenthetical commas that the man is 'even older than Noah's grandfather', and a variety of adjectives in addition to 'old' (like 'wrinkled' and 'elderly') are also used. Boyne also indicates that the brightness of the man's eyes and of his hair colour capture the boy's attention. The metaphor 'mop' has connotations of messiness but also creates a pleasing impression of a rather gentle, loveable character. These aspects of his appearance suggest that despite his age, the toymaker is young at heart and perhaps also that he's rather eccentric. His language supports an overall impression of kindness and approachability, for example his repeated use of the phrase 'oh dear'. But there is clearly more to him than just a kindly old man; what the toymaker says about the footsteps and the doorbell are rather strange, and strongly suggest that things are not quite as they seem where the toyshop and its owner are concerned.

This precise and sophisticated impression acts as an overview for the evidence that follows.

Relevant quotation is used to support the point.

This evidence is explored by drawing an inference from the language used.

Another accurate impression is noted and a strong choice of quotations is selected to support it.

Reference to language techniques is made throughout.

A further impression is noted as a summary of the evidence given earlier.

Another impression and supporting evidence is offered.

Concludes with an overall summary linking back to the introductory sentence.

Comment on Response 2

This answer makes a strong initial point, supports this with textual evidence, and goes on to make further linked and detailed points. Comments are detailed and make reference to language and literary techniques such as adjectives, repetition and metaphor, although more could be made of sentence level features and aspects of the text's structure. However, the effects of some language and literary techniques are written about in a fluent, extended and insightful way.

What you have achieved

Reading

- You have identified and understood explicit information about characters and inferred additional information.

- You have identified effective words and phrases in character descriptions.

- You have commented on the way that writers use vocabulary and language techniques to create convincing characters.

Writing

- You have used a variety of techniques to build and develop character.

- You have chosen vocabulary and imagery that is varied, imaginative and powerful.

- You have varied the length and style of your sentences, and used a variety of punctuation, to create different effects in your descriptions.

Speaking and listening

- You have been able to vary speech, gesture and movement in your presentation of a character.

- You have built up detail in your performances to convey character.

- You have listened carefully and focused on detail in response to what you have seen and heard.

Next steps

Reading
Read a variety of fiction and non-fiction, including feature articles and interviews. Across all your wider reading, think about how effectively characters are described: are they rounded, complex, convincing, memorable? How has this been achieved? How do they change and develop?

Writing
You have written about a superhero; now try writing about a villain, and reveal aspects of your character's true nature throughout your description. You could also write up your improvised script, including stage directions, or complete the descriptive self-portrait.

Speaking and listening
Continue to think about how character is conveyed in drama through tone of voice, body language, gesture, facial expression and movement, as well as through the words themselves. Improvise new short scenes with a partner or read drama texts, noticing how the playwright has provided clues about characters in both the dialogue and the stage directions.

Chapter 2 Explaining

Great inventions

What's it all about?

This chapter focuses on texts that provide explanations. You will read explanatory leaflets, articles, blogs and webpages about inventions such the wheel, the telephone, the bike, satellites and driverless cars. You will look at how explanatory texts are put together and learn how to shape and write an article of your own.

You should already know:
- the differences between formal and informal language
- how to summarise ideas and information from a text
- how to organise your own writing to make your meaning clear
- how to deliver an effective presentation to engage the listener.

You will learn how to:
- gather together and summarise information and ideas from two texts
- explain why a writer uses formal and informal language
- deliberately use a variety of sentence types and punctuation (including colons and semicolons) for various effects
- plan and deliver a presentation, thinking carefully about how it can be supported by visual aids.

You will:
- plan and deliver a short presentation on an imagined invention
- write an engaging article on a recent invention
- write a summary of two texts about the invention of the bicycle and answer questions about them.

Enjoy reading

You will learn how to:
- share your first impressions of an explanatory text
- work out what the text is about and why it has been written.

You are going to read an extract taken from a blog called 'Things I learned from riding in a Google self-driving car'.

1 Think about the title of the blog.

a) What is a 'self-driving car'?

b) What do you think the writer might have learned?

c) Do you think all cars will be 'self-driving' in the future?

2 Read the extract slowly, noting down any words you do not know.

Things I learned from riding in a Google self-driving car

Last week, a friend and I got a sneak peek at Google's new self-driving cars. In addition [...] I got to chat with the engineers about the project. [...]

It's not done and it's not perfect.

Some of the scenarios autonomous vehicles have the most trouble with are 5
the scenarios *human beings* have the most trouble with, such as traversing
four-way stops or handling a yellow light (do you brake suddenly, or floor it
and run the light?). At one point during the trip, we were attempting to
make a right turn onto a busy road. Everyone's attention was directed to the
left, waiting for an opening. When the road cleared and it was safe to turn 10
right, the car didn't budge. I thought this was a bug at first, but when I
looked to my right there was a pedestrian standing very close to the curb,
giving the awkward body language that he was planning on **jaywalking**.
This was a very human interaction: the car was waiting for a further visual
cue from the pedestrian to either stop or go, and the pedestrian waiting for a 15
cue from the car. When the pedestrian didn't move, the self-driving car
gracefully took the lead, merged, and entered the roadway.

Freaky.

The cars use a mixture of 3D laser-mapping, GPS, and radar to analyse and
interpret their surroundings, and the latest versions are fully electric with a 20
range of about 100 miles. The radar is interesting because it allows the car to
see through objects, rather than relying on line-of-sight. At one point during
our drive the car recognised and halted for a cyclist who was concealed
behind a row of hedges.

Despite the advantages over a human being in certain scenarios, however, 25
these cars still aren't ready for the real world. They can't drive in the snow or
heavy rain, and there's a variety of complex situations they do not process

---

well, such as passing through a construction zone. Google is hoping with enough logged miles and data, eventually the cars will be able to handle all of this as well (or better) than a human could. [...] 30

It wasn't an exhilarating ride, and that's a good thing.

Riding in a self-driving car is not the white-knuckled, cybernetic thrill ride one might expect. The car drives like a person, and after a few minutes you forget that you're being driven autonomously. You forget that a robot is differentiating cars from pedestrians from mopeds from raccoons. You 35 forget that millions of photons are being fired from a laser and interpreting, processing, and reacting to the hand signals of a cyclist. You forget that instead of an organic brain, which has had millions of years to evolve the cognitive ability to fumble its way through a four-way stop, you're being piloted by an artificial one, which was birthed in less than a decade. 40

From www.theoatmeal.com

3 Now choose five of the words you noted down. Can you work out what each one means?

   a) What sort of word is it: a verb, adjective, adverb or noun?

   b) Does it contain a prefix or suffix you know already? (For example, 'im' is a prefix meaning 'not'.)

   c) Does the context help? Look at the rest of the sentence – what is happening?

4 Note down answers to the following big five questions.

   a) **Who** has written this extract?

   b) **What** is being described in the extract?

   c) **When** are the events happening – now or in the past or future?

   d) **Where** do the events take place?

   e) **Why** has the writer written this text?

5 What did you enjoy or find interesting about the extract?

6 This extract is from a type of writing called a blog. It is usually a personal piece of online writing and is often written in an *informal, conversational style*. Find a phrase or sentence which shows that this is a blog.

7 Have you ever read anything like this before? Is it the kind of writing you would normally read? Why? Why not?

Vocabulary

jaywalking: crossing a street unlawfully or without paying attention to traffic

What is writing to explain?

You will learn how to:
- recognise and comment on the common features of explanatory texts.

Explanatory texts help the reader to understand a process or how something works. They can also give reasons for why something is like it is. As texts are often written to achieve more than one purpose, it is likely that explanatory texts will provide information and some may also entertain.

Explore

There are many different types of explanatory texts, such as leaflets, articles, encyclopedias, and posters.

Read the leaflet opposite and answer these questions.

1 What is the leaflet explaining?

2 Who do you think the leaflet is aimed at? How do you know?

MRI – Magnetic Resonance Imaging

Hi there, I'm Mr Mole!

I'm here to tell you all about your MRI examination.

MRI is a way of looking inside your body without using X-rays.

MRI is **very** safe.

Magnetic Resonance Imaging uses:
- A very large magnet
- Radio waves
- A computer

The MRI scanner looks like a big [tunnel] with a hole in the middle where the magnet is. It is very light and airy and you will have plenty of room.

MRI works like this:
- You will lie on the scanner table and slide slowly into the scanner. You may go in head first or feet first depending on what we are scanning.

- The magnet is always on.
- We use radio waves to make the pictures. When we turn these on and off they make lots of noise.
- The computer turns the magnet's signal into a picture.

From www.wsh.nhs.uk

This text explains the process of an MRI scan in a clear and simple way. This will reassure its young readers and help them to understand how it works.

3 The following features in the leaflet help to explain the process clearly. Find an example for each one and explain how it helps makes the leaflet clear for the reader.

a) heading

b) subheading

c) bullet points

d) simple vocabulary

e) **simple sentences**

Develop

Explanation texts focus on processes or causes and effects.

The text below is about how cinema began. It is taken from an information board in a museum exhibition.

4 Rearrange the five sections into order. Use the **connectives** or **topic sentences** at the beginning of the paragraphs to help you.

1

> **Following Roget's discovery,** it did not take people long to notice that a moving image could be created. Scientists from all over the world, therefore, tried to develop a variety of devices for creating this illusion of the moving image.

2

> **How Cinema was Invented**

3

> **The story of cinema began in 1824.** Peter Roget, an English doctor, was the first to identify something he called 'persistence vision': if we see a series of objects in similar position in a rapid sequence, our eyes tend to see a single moving object.

Key term

simple sentence: a sentence that contains one subject and one verb (e.g. 'The bell rang.')

Key terms

connective: a linking word or phrase used in a sentence (e.g. 'and', 'but', 'or', 'so', 'then', 'because', 'after')

topic sentence: a sentence in a paragraph – usually at the beginning – that shows the reader the main subject of the writing

4

> **And so** a wonderful new art form was born: cinema.

5

> **However**, the first successful public showing of moving images, created by cinematography, was not until the 1890s. Auguste and Louis Lumière, two French brothers, created a combined camera and projector called the Cinématographe. It recorded the pictures on a strip made out of celluloid (thin transparent plastic) which passed through a shutter at 16 frames per second.

5 What makes this an explanation text?

6 The text focuses on some of the technical aspects of how cinema was invented. The writer has therefore used some technical or specialist words and phrases (e.g. 'shutter', which is a device on a camera).

   a) Find two further examples of technical or specialist words and phrases.

   b) How has the writer tried to clarify some of the words and phrases for the non-specialist reader?

Respond

The extract below explains how the wheel was invented. It is taken from a children's history book. Read the extract and answer the questions that follow.

The Invention of the Wheel

The wheel is, famously, one of the most important inventions in the history of mankind: without wheels, there would be no bikes, no cars, no longer journeys, even no heavy machines (they use wheels – or gears – inside).

Logs

Before wheels, if you wanted to move something really massive then you'd need some logs and many, many people. You'd put the logs on the ground and roll your massive object on top of them. It must have been slow and absolutely exhausting!

Axles

Then somebody, somewhere, at some point in time (about 5000 years ago in the Middle East, actually) had a brilliant idea: attach a wheel to an axle. An axle is a shaft on, or attached to, a revolving wheel or pair of wheels. It takes less energy to turn the axle than to turn the wheel. These were first attached to simple carts and pulled by animals. Much less exhausting – for humans, anyway!

Spokes

After the axle was invented, the wheels were still made out of solid wood. Then somebody, somewhere, at some point in time (about 4000 years ago in Siberia, actually) had a brilliant idea: use spokes inside the wheel to replace the solid wood. The wheels were lighter and therefore faster. I suppose the next thing that needed to be invented was some brakes!

7   Identify the features of an explanatory text used in this extract.

8   Some writers of explanatory texts want to entertain their readers as well. How has the writer of this text made the explanation humorous and engaging for the reader? Consider:

- use of informal language
- repetition
- humour.

Exploring how explanations are structured

You will learn how to:
- identify and comment on the ways an explanatory text can be organised for clarity.

Explanatory texts are carefully organised in order to make the explanation clear and easy to follow.

Explore

Read the following text. It is taken from the NASA website.

What Is a Satellite?

Why Are Satellites Important?

The bird's-eye view that satellites have allows them to see large areas of Earth at one time. This ability means satellites can collect more data, more quickly, than instruments on the ground.

Satellites also can see into space better than telescopes at Earth's surface. That's because satellites fly above the clouds, dust and molecules in the atmosphere that can block the view from ground level.

Before satellites, TV signals didn't go very far. TV signals only travel in straight lines. So they would quickly trail off into space instead of following Earth's curve. Sometimes mountains or tall buildings would block them. [...]

With satellites, TV signals and phone calls are sent upward to a satellite. Then, almost instantly, the satellite can send them back down to different locations on Earth.

What Are the Parts of a Satellite?

Satellites come in many shapes and sizes. But most have at least two parts in common – an antenna and a power source. The antenna sends and receives information, often to and from Earth. The power source can be a solar panel or battery. Solar panels make power by turning sunlight into electricity.

From www.nasa.gov

1. Put the topics covered in this extract in order.

   A They have antenna and power sources.

   B Satellites can see large areas.

   C They are better than TV signals.

   D They can look deep into space.

2   Writers use a number of techniques to structure explanatory texts. Which of these features can you spot in the extract?

- presentation features, such as headings and subheadings
- topic sentences

Connectives can help to provide a structure for an explanatory text in different ways.

They can indicate cause and effect. For example: *because*, *so*, *as a result*, *therefore*, *since*, *due to*.

For example, the highlighted 'So' in the extract is connecting a cause (TV signals can only travel in straight lines) with an effect (they trail off into space because of Earth's curve).

They can show a sequence. For example: *next*, *then*, *after*, *before*, *eventually*.

For example, the highlighted 'Then' connects the sequence of the signal going up into space and back down again.

3   Find an example of the following:

a) a *cause and effect* connective

b) a *sequencing* connective.

Topic sentences help the reader to understand the subject of the rest of the paragraph. For example, the topic sentence in the second paragraph is: 'Satellites also can see into space better than telescopes at Earth's surface.' Like the example, topic sentences are often *simple sentences*.

4   The paragraph below continues the extract. The topic sentence has been removed. Write a topic sentence for the paragraph. Ensure it is a simple sentence.

> _____. Sometimes these instruments point toward Earth to gather information about its land, air and water. Other times they face toward space to collect data from the solar system and universe.

Respond

5   Write a summary of the features of satellites. Use the topic sentences and subheadings to help you.

Using formal and informal language in explanation texts

You will learn how to:
- identify and comment on the use of formal and informal language.

The style of language writers choose depends on their audience and purpose.

Explore

Writers may choose to write either formally or informally for a number of reasons. An online blog explaining scientific ideas to a general audience is more likely to be informal, whereas a science report that will be read by a specialist scientific community is more likely to be formal.

Writers may choose a formal style to add seriousness or authority; an informal style may help the text to sound lively and engaging.

1　Note down whether each of these features is more likely to be found in a formal or an informal text.

a) conversational phrases (e.g. 'okay')

b) longer, complex sentences

c) slang (e.g. 'kid' for 'child')

d) contractions (e.g. 'that's')

e) expressive punctuation, such as an exclamation mark to express an attitude (e.g. 'Wow!')

f) sentence fragments/minor sentences (e.g. 'Unbelievable.')

g) technical or specialist vocabulary

h) sentences beginning with the conjunctions 'or', 'and' or 'but'

i) precise vocabulary

Develop

2　Imagine you have been asked to write the following texts. For each text, explain whether you would adopt a formal or informal style. Consider the form, audience and purposes of each text.

a) a leaflet aimed at children about inventors

b) an email to an investment group asking them to fund the manufacture of a new invention

c) an online guide about how to use a new smartphone.

Read this entry from an adult encyclopedia.

Text A

The first *papermaking* process was documented in China during the *Eastern Han* period (25–220 CE), and is traditionally attributed to the court official *Ts'ai Lun* (c. 50–121 CE). He is credited with the invention of a type of paper made of mulberry and other plant fibres, along with fishing nets and old rags, which reduced the cost of paper production. Although Ts'ai Lun became very wealthy and famous in China, it took many centuries for his papermaking process to spread to other countries and continents.

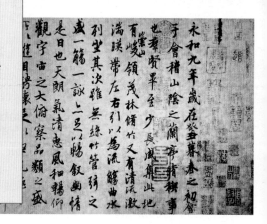

3   What features of Text A help to make it formal?

4   Why has the writer of Text A adopted a formal style?

Respond

Read this extract from a museum guide aimed at children.

Text B

Before paper was invented, people used to drag around massive books made out of wood or spend a lot on expensive silk. But legend tells of a man called Ts'ai Lun. He was a court official in China over two thousand years ago and he cooked up a funky recipe. He took a bit of tree bark, chucked in some bamboo plant, and threw in some rags and fishing nets he had lying around. He then mashed it all into a pulp and invented paper. Lightweight and cheap. And people didn't need to haul around huge wooden books any more. Ts'ai Lun made a lot of money (not paper money though – that wasn't invented until 800 years later!) but it took hundreds of years for the secrets of papermaking to catch on in other countries.

Uses informal, conversational vocabulary.

Sentences beginning with a conjunction.

5   Find more examples of informal language features.

6   Explain why the writer adopted a largely informal style.

7   Which of the two versions – Text A or Text B – do you prefer and why?

Collating and summarising information from two texts

You will learn how to:
- identify relevant information from two texts
- collate and synthesise information to write a concise summary.

The ability to summarise is a valuable skill. Sometimes you need to read more than one text in order to write a comprehensive summary of a topic.

Explore

The activities in this unit will help you complete this summary task:

Write a summary of how the pedal bicycle was invented.

Read Text A below about the invention of the pedal bicycle.

Text A

> Pierre Lallement, a Frenchman, probably invented the first successful pedal-driven bicycle. He was born on 25 October 1843. Before reaching the age of 20, he was already a highly regarded maker of baby carriages, which gave him the skills needed to design the first bicycle. His main inspiration involved adding a rotating mechanism and pedals to the hub of the front wheel. Early bikes were very uncomfortable due to their stiff and heavy iron frames and wooden wheels wrapped with an iron rim. They therefore became known as *boneshakers*.

A student has written a list of points from Text A on how the bicycle was invented.

- Pierre Lallement probably invented the first pedal bicycle in 1864.
- He was born on 25 October 1843.
- He applied his skills as a maker of baby carriages.
- He added a rotating mechanism and pedals.
- Early bikes were uncomfortable and were known as boneshakers.

1. Which points above are not relevant for the summary task on how the pedal bicycle was invented?

Now read Text B, which is also about the invention of the pedal bicycle.

Text B

[A] story about the invention of the bicycle credits Pierre Lallement as being the 'father of the bicycle.' Reportedly, in 1862, while in **Nancy** he noticed someone riding a **draisienne** and saw the rider was required to propel the vehicle by walking. Lallement modified the draisienne by attaching pedals and adding a rotary crank mechanism. In 1863, Lallement moved to Paris and interacted with the Oliviers, who then formed a partnership with Pierre Michaux to build a bicycle.

From www.geriwalton.com

2 Using the example above to help you, write a list of points from Text B about how the pedal bicycle was invented.

Develop

When summarising information from two texts, you should first look for any information that is repeated across both texts and combine it into one point.

3 Look at the two lists and see if any points could be combined in this way. Write out the sentence with the phrase 'Both texts…' at the beginning.

Note that some points are only in Text A and others only in Text B. When summarising, indicate which text a point comes from. When writing your summary, be concise and use your own words as much as you can. For example, the sentence 'A story about the invention of the bicycle credits Pierre Lallement as being the "father of the bicycle."' could be summarised as 'It is thought that Pierre Lallement invented the bicycle.'

4 Choose a point from your list in Question 3 and write it more concisely.

Respond

5 Write a summary of how the pedal bicycle was invented. Write no more than 50 words.

Vocabulary

Nancy: a city in France

draisienne: a type of early bicycle in which the rider paddled their feet against the ground.

Checklist for success

✔ Ensure all points are relevant to the focus of the task.

✔ Combine points where possible.

✔ Use your own words and be as concise as possible.

✔ Indicate which text the information is from: both texts, Text A or Text B.

Explaining things clearly in speech and presentations

You will learn how to:
- shape a short presentation using appropriate media, and answer questions
- adjust your pace to maintain the listener's interest.

People who give effective explanatory presentations and thoughtful responses to questions do three things: plan well, consider the needs of their audience and listen carefully.

Imagine you are an inventor. You have been asked to give a presentation about a life-changing invention you have made. After the presentation, you will answer questions.

1 Decide what your invention will be (a medicine or a machine perhaps) and make notes on what you will say about:

a) what your invention is

b) how and why it works

c) what its benefits are to individuals and society

d) how much it will cost to develop.

2 Decide on the best order for the information you want to present. Then write a short, simple topic sentence statement to introduce each point. For example:

> *eTranslator uses the latest cutting-edge technology.*

You should then consider ways to develop each point by giving more information. You could include:

- anecdotes
- facts and opinions
- expert views.

Think also about how to make your points interesting. The example below uses an anecdote, **rhetorical question** and **rule of three** and is therefore more likely to engage the audience.

> I went on holiday last week but I really struggled to communicate with the guard on a train – we didn't have a single word in common! It took a very long time for me to get the ticket. But can you imagine a world where people from across the globe, all speaking different languages, can easily communicate? Now you can. eTranslator will connect people, develop friendships and build bridges across nations.

Key terms

rhetorical question: a question that is used to make people think, rather than requiring an answer

rule of three: a useful pattern of three examples, which makes the information or idea expressed memorable

3 Now develop each of your statements to add interest. Use the example above to help you.

4 Come up with a memorable ending to your presentation. For example:

> Developing eTranslator will cost a few thousand, but it will transform many millions of lives.

Visual aids can help illustrate explanations. Choose images carefully and make sure they help you to communicate your ideas. Avoid including lots of words on any handouts or presentation slides.

For example, if your invention is designed to help improve traffic in busy cities, you could include an image of a congested city street with the heading: 'Is this what you want your future to be like?' Or you could add a chart showing the increase in the number of car journeys.

Is this what you want your future to be like?

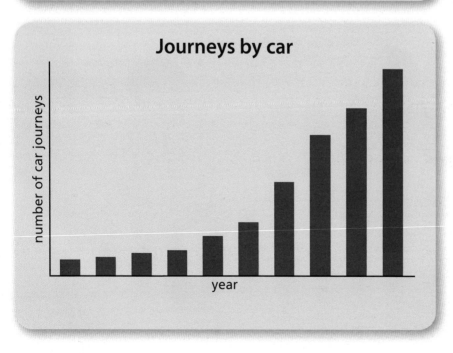

Journeys by car

number of car journeys

year

5 **a)** Which of the features below do you think would be suitable for your presentation?

- images
- headings
- charts and diagrams
- short video clips

b) Where appropriate, add suitable visual aids to your presentation plan.

6 Rehearse your presentation.

a) Practise changing the **pace** of what you say. You could, for example, slow down when you are giving any difficult or technical explanations.

b) Pause to highlight a point and keep your listener's interest.

c) Speak loudly and clearly.

> **Key term**
> ....
> **pace:** the speed at which you speak

Respond

7 Take turns to give your presentation.

8 After each presentation, the listeners should ask questions to find out more about the invention. When replying to questions:

- use the question's words in your answer
- keep your response relevant and concise.

9 As listeners, give feedback to explain how the speaker could improve their presentation. Consider the following:

a) Does every point make sense? What could be clearer?

b) What extra information might the listener want to know?

c) What could make the talk more interesting?

d) Did the visual aids help to clarify and communicate the points being made?

e) Was the talk organised throughout? Were there any points where the talk moved too far away from the topic?

f) Was there anything you didn't understand? Could the speaker have reworded any sections by breaking them down into simpler sentences?

Planning a report

You will learn how to:
- plan the structure and content of a report
- consider audience, purpose and formality.

When you write a report, you need to plan how to organise information and explain your ideas clearly. This will ensure that your readers get the full picture but also know where to find specific information.

Explore

You are going to plan a formal report explaining and promoting a breakthrough invention that you would like to be taken into development. The intended audience is business leaders. You can use the idea you came up with for Unit 2.6 or think of a new one. Your report should answer any questions that readers might like to know about your invention. For example:

Title	eTranslator
Introduction	What is the invention?
	What is its most important benefit?
Middle (each paragraph will focus on a different question)	How does it work?
	Who would use it?
	What are its advantages?
	What are its disadvantages?
	How much will it cost to develop?
	How expensive will it be to buy and use?
Conclusion	Why should it be made?

1. Plan your report using a grid like the one above. Leave plenty of space to note your answers to each question. You may need to change the questions to suit your invention.

2. Decide on the best order for the questions in the middle section of your report. Number your points in that order.

3. Make a note of the points you will write to answer each question. Remember, you do not need to write in complete sentences in a plan – an example is given on the next page.

> Introduction
>
> What is the invention?
> - eTranslator
> - small device attaches to ear
> - automatically translates over 50 languages
>
> What is its most important benefit?
> - ease of communication across the globe

Develop

Reports often have subheadings to help readers find information easily. You can turn the questions in the middle section of your report into subheadings. For example, you can replace **pronouns** with proper nouns: so 'How does *it* work?' becomes 'How does *eTranslator* work?'.

Key term

pronoun: a word used instead of a noun, such as 'he', 'she', 'it', 'they', 'we', 'I', 'you'

4 Turn all the questions in your middle section into subheadings by using more precise vocabulary.

5 Write a full paragraph plan for two of your middle paragraphs, following the example below.

   a) Write a topic sentence summing up what the paragraph will tell readers.

   b) Note the more detailed explanation or evidence you will include. For example:

> **Topic sentence:** *eTranslator can be easily attached to your ear.*
> **Explanation and/or evidence:**
> - weighs 2 grams
> - uses magnetic technology
> - attaches behind the ear lobe
> - stylish design

Respond

6 Now complete all the paragraph plans for your report. Remember that the intended audience is business leaders, and that you should consider the appropriate level of formality.

Checklist for success

✔ Write a topic sentence expressing what each paragraph is about.

✔ Note the details you will include in each paragraph.

Using connectives to explain clearly

You will learn how to:
- use adverbial clauses
- choose connectives to explain information clearly.

You need to use connectives to show how information, details and ideas link together in a piece of explanatory writing. This will help to guide readers through your text. Adverbial clauses provide more information in a sentence about how or when something is done.

Explore

The grid below shows the connectives you can use to create **adverbial clauses**. These can be used for different purposes.

Connectives	Purpose
because, since, for, as, for this reason	introduce a reason
to, in order to, in order for, so as to, so that	introduce a purpose
so, so that, as a result, with the result that	introduce a result
when, while, before, after	explain timing

Key term

adverbial clause: a group of words that tells us more about how or when an action is done, e.g. *'Before I go to bed*, I brush my teeth'

Read the following text.

> Robodriver will transform the way people travel because everyone in the car is able to enjoy being a passenger. As a result, everyone arrives at their destination feeling rested. Robodriver could be used when people travel to school or work, so that, on arrival, they will be able to achieve their best. Every year, thousands of accidents are caused by tired drivers. Using Robodriver would prevent those, since a robot never gets 'tired' – unlike every human.

This adverbial clause introduces a reason.

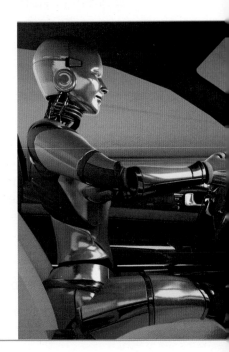

1 Find four other adverbial clauses in the text. Which of the four purposes from the grid does each one have?

Connectives can be used to create adverbial clauses. In the following example, the second clause is a *result* of the information in the first clause. So, you could use 'because', 'since' or 'for', but 'because' makes the best sense in this sentence.

> Driving yourself anywhere could become a thing of the past *because* Robodriver is so much safer.

2 Decide what type of connective should go in the gaps to link the ideas or details within the sentences. Should it be one showing reason, purpose or result?

a) Elderly people will have happier lives … Robodriver can take them to the shops, doctors, friends – no matter how frail they have become.

b) Robodriver can take young people to a destination without an adult being present … family life will be easier.

c) Vulnerable people will invest in Robodriver … they can travel safely.

d) … of Robodriver, people could work on their journey … they have to spend less time away from home.

Develop

Once you have decided *how* your next detail links with the previous one, you need to choose the best connective to make the link clear.

3 Write out the sentences in Question 2, adding a connective to make the meaning clear.

Respond

4 Write the first three paragraphs of an explanation of your invention for a young audience in a school assembly. Use connectives and adverbial clauses to link the information clearly.

Checklist for success

✔ Decide what the connection is between the ideas and information you are expressing.

✔ Use the best connective to express this link.

Varying sentence structure to make explanations clear and engaging

You will learn how to:
- use a mixture of simple, compound and complex sentences
- vary sentence structures to make explanations engaging.

Using different sentence structures allows you to express your ideas clearly and makes your writing interesting for your readers.

Explore

A short, simple sentence can make an important point clear for readers, especially if later sentences are longer, detailed or complex. For example:

> Robodriver is simple to use. It is affordable. It plugs straight into the car's ignition.

subject
verb
opinion
fact

Some explanatory texts might also require you to entertain your readers. Using three short sentences in a row here builds up all the advantages to impress readers.

1   Write three short, simple sentences explaining how your favourite gadget works. Use both fact and opinion.

Simple sentences can be useful to introduce a point or for impact. However, too many simple sentences can make your writing seem boring and simplistic.

Compound sentences are created by joining two or more main clauses with 'and', 'but' or 'or'. In the following example, 'and' emphasises the number of advantages and suggests that the last one may be surprising:

> Robodriver is simple to use and it is affordable.

Here, 'but' suggests that the second clause is unexpected and therefore of special interest to readers:

> Robodriver is cutting-edge technology but it is very simple to use.

In this example, 'or' suggests there is a range of exciting possibilities:

> Robodriver can take the kids to school or it can take you to work.

2. Look at these compound sentences. Choose a connective for each of the gaps that would impress readers with the advantages of using Robodriver.

> Robodriver allows employees to travel long distances ... feel ready to work as soon as they arrive. They can work during the journey ... when they are in the office.

3. Write three compound sentences about the advantages of your favourite gadget. Craft each sentence with a different connective to create a specific positive effect on your reader.

To make an explanation clearer or more interesting, you can include extra information in a sentence using a pair of brackets, commas or dashes. Put this information directly after the word or phrase it is expanding on.

> Robodriver (designed in 2015) relies on a network of sensors, covering every surface, that measure speed, size and movement around the car. The control panel – a circular touchscreen – fits over the steering wheel.

Key term

compound sentence: a sentence that contains equally weighted simple sentences joined by connectives

4 Look at the grid below. Write out the three sentences and add the extra information so that it refers to the underlined word in the main clause.

Main clause	Extra information
In <u>tests</u> Robodriver was 100% successful.	carried out by independent experts
Robodriver's reaction time was <u>faster</u> than a racing driver's	by up to 100 times
<u>Passengers</u> reported feeling safe while being driven by Robodriver.	of all ages

5 Write three sentences about features of your favourite gadget that include interesting but additional, non-essential information.

To make your sentences even more varied, you can use **subordinating conjunctions** to create **complex sentences**. They can be useful for presenting ideas that need layers of information and details. Complex sentences can be particularly useful in an explanation because they can show cause and effect.

For example, a cause (everybody wants to feel safe) can be joined with its effects (millions will buy the invention) to form this complex sentence: 'This invention will sell millions *because* everybody wants to feel safe.'

Other subordinating conjunctions that show cause and effect include 'so', 'since', 'unless' and 'due to'.

6 Write three complex sentences about your favourite gadget that show cause and effect.

Key terms
....

subordinating conjunction: a word used to link clauses in a complex sentence (e.g. 'although', 'while', 'when', 'if')

complex sentence: a sentence that contains a supporting idea expressed in a subordinate clause, which adds to the information in the main idea expressed in the main clause

When you write a paragraph, decide how to use different types of sentences to make your meaning clear and engage your reader. For example:

> Robodriver is better than sat nav. A sat nav is only as good as the driver and it does not help drivers avoid dangers. However, Robodriver has sensors which notice what other cars are doing so not only can it follow a map, it can also swerve out of the way of another car. That's got to be safer!

A short, simple sentence expressing the main point ensures readers notice it.

A compound sentence provides more detail.

A complex sentence offers supporting ideas and shows cause and effect.

A short sentence at the end of the paragraph emphasises the conclusion.

7 Write a paragraph comparing your favourite gadget to a similar one. Explain why you prefer yours. Include examples and comparisons, and use a variety of connectives. Vary your use of sentence types for effect.

Respond

8 Write two paragraphs for an engaging online article explaining how a gadget in your home works. Make sure you use a variety of sentence structures for effect.

Checklist for success

✔ Organise simple, compound and complex sentences for effect.

✔ Position information in your sentences and choose connectives to engage your readers.

Using colons and semicolons to include more detail

You will learn how to:

- use a colon to introduce a list, example, reason or conclusion
- use a semicolon to separate items in a list or closely linked sentences.

You can make your explanatory writing more sophisticated by using colons and **semicolons** for particular effects.

> **Explore**

A colon can be used to introduce a list of items. It is placed before the first item in the list:

> The technology I use most often is: a computer, telephone, washing machine and microwave.

Key term

semicolon (;): used to connect two independent clauses (clauses that could each be a sentence on their own)

1 Write a sentence listing the five best inventions of all time. Use a colon.

A colon can also emphasise a conclusion or explanation. The statement before the colon must make sense on its own:

> Many inventions are not essential: they are luxuries. The popcorn maker is not needed: it is easier to make popcorn in a saucepan or microwave.

In the first sentence, the colon emphasises the conclusion. In the second sentence, it emphasises the explanation.

2 Which of these explanations can be rewritten using a colon?

   a) The invention of the light bulb took many years. Thomas Edison made hundreds that did not work.

   b) It is easier to invent a new flavour of cake. I love trying out new flavours.

3 Write two sentences about the topic 'What makes a great invention?' One sentence should introduce an explanation, the other a conclusion.

When you have longer items in a list, you should use semicolons to separate the items. For example:

> Inventions I could not live without include: a hairdryer; my special pair of running shoes; and chocolate-coated biscuits.

4 Write a sentence that includes a list needing a semicolon about life-saving inventions.

A semicolon can also replace a full stop, to separate two sentences whose meaning is linked. This emphasises the closeness more strongly than a connective would. For example:

> 3D printing can create interesting-looking food; it cannot make it taste nice.

5 Could you use a semicolon to link these sentences? Explain why or why not.

a) Wind-up radios save energy. In remote places, they also keep you connected with the news.

b) Use your GravityLight to generate electricity through weight. Fill the small bag with rocks or sand.

6 Write two sentences linked with a semicolon.

Respond

7 Describe a new toy for younger children, using colons and semicolons to introduce information and to punctuate lists correctly.

Checklist for success

✔ Use a colon to introduce a list, example, reason or conclusion.

✔ Use a semicolon to emphasise the close meaning of two sentences or to separate longer list items.

Writing your own explanatory article

You will learn how to:
- combine the informative writing skills you have learned in one text
- understand what makes a high-level piece of informative writing.

Your task

Write an engaging online article commenting on the impact an invention is having. The invention can be real or imaginary.

Some ideas include:

- smart meters for electricity use in the home
- electric bicycles
- 3D printing
- satellite navigation devices.

Approaching the task

1 Decide what invention you are going to write about, then plan your ideas using a grid like the one below. Start by noting the questions readers might want answered in your article.

Section	Questions about the impact ... is having
Title (include the name of the invention)	
Introduction	How is this invention affecting people/improving things?
Middle (each paragraph will focus on a different question)	
Conclusion	

2 Plan each paragraph in turn.

   a) Write a sentence that sums up what the paragraph is about.

   b) Decide what details you will include in the paragraph.

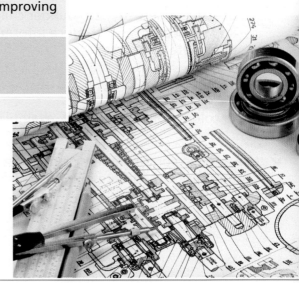

3 Consider how you could include some features of informal language in order to make your article lively and engaging.

4 Write your article or report, following your plan and crafting your sentences so that each one is clear, informative and engaging for your readers.

a) Include short, simple sentences and develop your explanations using compound and complex sentences. Look back at the connectives you have learned about in this chapter.

b) Use a colon to introduce a list or if you want to emphasise an explanation, example or conclusion. Do not use a colon in every sentence or it will lose its impact.

c) Remember to use a semicolon to separate items in a list if a comma is already being used in a description of an item.

d) At least once, craft two sentences close in meaning and use a semicolon between them to emphasise their connection.

5 When you have written your text, read it through, checking the following points.

Sentences:

- Does every sentence make sense?
- Does each sentence have the effect you want, or do you need to rewrite some of them? For example, would it be better to begin with a different clause? Are your simple sentences having impact, or are they so frequent they make your writing boring?
- Have you chosen the right type of connective each time?
- Have you written some sentences where the colon emphasises a reason, conclusion or example?
- Have you used a semicolon to separate a pair of sentences closely linked by meaning?

Punctuation in lists:

- Have you placed a colon before the beginning of a list?
- Have you used semicolons to separate longer list items?

Formality

- Have you used some informal language features effectively? Is the article engaging?

6 Compare your own response to the task to the two responses below. Using the comments, identify ways in which your own response could be improved and rewrite it, if needed.

Response 1

Running shoes that make you run faster have been a great success. All sorts of people are buying them: fitness enthusiasts, especially older runners; teenagers; and new runners. They are cheap and easy to use. As a result, schools are encouraging children who are often late to buy a pair so that when they have to run for the bus, they will actually catch it.

Athletes have found them very useful in training because the shoes can be set to run at different speeds. 'It lets my legs practise moving at a higher speed so I know what it feels like,' explained Olympic champion Mahmoud Ali. However, officials check every runner's shoes before each race in order to make sure no one is wearing a pair.

Uses a variety of sentence structures.

Punctuation is varied and accurate enough to make the meaning clear.

Some connectives are used to link sentences and clauses.

Comment on Response 1

The student uses features of the form, and the text suits its audience and purpose. The paragraphs begin with topic sentences and the content is relevant and developed in some detail. The information is organised logically and uses a variety of sentence structures and connectives. However, the report could have used some informal features to engage the readers.

Response 2

New 'Zero' is a hero!

Zero-calorie chocolate bars, called 'Zero', have made millions! Every day, customers are tucking into the delicious plain, dark chocolate; dark chocolate and ginger; or dark chocolate and mint bars. Sales figures are enormous because this snack will not add even a gram to your weight.

Amazingly, this popular invention was discovered by accident. The fruit of the lipo plant looks like a purple coconut. So, scientists wondered if its fruit had the same high levels of oil too. They did. However, there was one important difference: lipo 'oil' has zero calories. This led Dr Meyer of Indeberg to wonder if he could make low-calorie desserts.

'But when lipo was mixed with the zero-calorie sweetener, saccharine, it just hardened,' he explained. So he chucked the result in the bin. However, a cleaner joked that it looked like a white chocolate bar. As a result, the scientist tried adding chocolate flavouring and, suddenly, he had invented everyone's dream: a zero-calorie chocolate bar.

Uses a variety of sentence types to vary text and make writing interesting.

Features of informal language used to engage the reader.

Uses a variety of connectives to link sentences and clauses.

Makes accurate use of semicolons and colons.

Comment on Response 2

This student has sequenced paragraphs logically and has linked them clearly and purposefully. The sentences also show varied length and structure, and features of informal language will engage the reader. The writer is using the colon in different ways, but has only used the semicolon in lists. To improve this response, the student should position clauses and sentences to have an effect on readers, and use semicolons to emphasise connections.

Responding to a pair of explanation texts

You will learn how to:

- synthesise and summarise information from two explanation texts
- evaluate your summary and work to improve it.

The text below is an article from a technology website.

You are going to explore the ways in which both this article and the blog you read at the start of this chapter work, using the understanding you have built up in this chapter.

Google's driverless cars [...]

[...]

Google's driverless car has eight sensors.

The most noticeable is the rotating roof-top LiDAR – a camera that uses an array of 32 or 64 lasers to measure 5 the distance to objects to build up a 3D map at a range of 200 m, letting the car 'see' hazards.

The car also sports another set of 'eyes', a standard camera that points through the windscreen. This also looks for nearby hazards – such as pedestrians, cyclists 10 and other motorists – and reads road signs and detects traffic lights.

[...]

How Google's driverless car works

No single sensor is responsible for making Google's 15 self-driving car work... Instead, the driverless car uses data from all eight sensors, interpreted by Google's software, to keep you safe and get you from A to B.

The data that Google's software receives is used to accurately identify other road users and their behaviour 20 patterns, plus commonly used highway signals.

For example, the Google car can successfully identify a bike and understand that if the cyclist extends an arm, they intend to make a manoeuvre.

From www.alphr.com

Understanding the text

1 Read the article 'Google's driverless cars'.

   a) What functions does the standard camera have?

   b) How is the data that is received by Google's software used?

Thinking about the text's purpose and features

2 Which aspects of explanatory writing can you identify in the article 'Google's driverless cars'? Copy and complete the grid with relevant line numbers or a brief quotation.

Features of explanatory text	Line number or brief quotation
heading	
subheading	
technical or specialist vocabulary	
technical or specialist vocabulary explained for a non-specialist reader	
short sentences and paragraphs for clarity	
serious, formal tone	

Looking at the text in detail

Now look again at the blog 'Things I learned from riding in a Google Self-driving Car' on pages 42–43.

3 The driverless car is described in the final sentence as being 'birthed in less than a decade'. What does the writer find surprising about the development of the technology?

4 The writer uses an informal minor sentence in its own paragraph: 'Freaky.'

   a) What does he find so unsettling?

   b) What are the effects on the reader of using this informal language feature?

5 Find the colon in the second paragraph. Does this emphasise a conclusion or an explanation?

6 Look again at the article 'Google's driverless cars'. Make a list of what you learn about how the driverless car works.

Here is an example to help you:

> It has a standard camera that identifies hazards, road signs and traffic lights.

7 Now read the blog, 'Things I learned from riding in a Google Self-driving Car' on pages 42–43 and make a list of what you learn about how driverless cars work. Here is an example to help you:

> millions of photons are fired from a laser, which reacts to human behaviour

8 Based on your reading of the blog and the article, write a summary of what you learn about how Google's driverless cars work. Write no more than 50 words.

- Bring together the two lists you created for questions 6 and 7; see if any of your points could be combined (for example, you could combine any information about the laser into one point).

- There is no need to compare the two texts for this task, although you could specify which text the point came from (the blog or the article).

- When writing your summary, remember to be concise and use your own words as much as you can.

- Make sure your focus is on *how the driverless cars work* and include only what you consider to be the most important information.

9 Compare your own response to Question 8 to the two below. Once you have read them, identify ways in which your own response could be improved. Rewrite it, if needed.

Response 1

The cars use a mixture of 3D laser-mapping, GPS and radar to analyse their surroundings and they have a rotating roof-top LiDAR which uses lasers to see hazards – it can even see through objects. All of this technology produces data that is interpreted by software and used to understand the behaviour of other road users. The blog says Google is hoping to log all this data so eventually their cars can handle complex situations as well as, or better than, a human.

This section could be improved by not copying word for word.

The first sentence is rather long and lacks the concision required by a summary.

This sentence is an effective summary and the student is beginning to use more of their own words.

This detail is inaccurate and unnecessary.

Comment on Response 1

This is a good attempt to summarise. The points are all relevant to the focus of the task and the student sensibly handles both texts. However, the answer relies on copying phrases and sentences directly from the texts rather than concisely combining and summarising the ideas. It also includes additional details that aren't required (for example, 'as well as, or better than, a human').

Response 2

Both texts say that driverless cars combine a range of different sensors, from cameras to cutting-edge rotating lasers on the roof which can see through objects. The article says this technology creates data which is interpreted by software to understand hazards and human behaviour and drive accordingly. The blog says data from all driverless cars is logged and used to improve their ability to respond safely to more complex situations.

Rather than listing all the technology, the student has selected the main information (cameras and lasers).

The student identifies the sources of the different pieces of information.

The response has avoided just copying words from the texts.

Comment on Response 2

This is a largely concise and relevant response which combines the main ideas from both texts. The response does not just copy phrases from the texts but instead effectively summarises how driverless cars work. However, the second sentence lacks concision and could be more carefully crafted.

What you have achieved

Reading

- You have identified and explained features of explanatory texts.

- You have commented on the ways an explanatory texts can be shaped and organised.

- You have identified and explained features of formal and informal language.

Writing

- You have planned and shaped the content of a report.

- You have used adverbial clauses and chosen connectives to explain information clearly.

- You have varied sentences to make your explanations more engaging.

- You have used colons and semicolons for particular effects.

Speaking and listening

- You have planned and shaped a short presentation.

- You have selected appropriate media to support your presentation.

- You have considered how to vary the pace of your delivery to maintain the listener's interest.

Next steps

Reading
Extend your reading and understanding of formal and informal language by looking at leaflets, manuals and posters to see if they use any surprising features of informal language. Look also at how different explanatory texts can have multiple purposes, such as to inform and to entertain.

Writing
Extend your explanatory writing skills by writing about an activity you know well, such as a sport or game. Write an explanation of how the activity works for somebody who has never seen or played it before. Think about how best to shape your explanation and how to use formal and informal language features depending on your chosen audience.

Speaking and listening
Extend your presentation skills by experimenting further with different visual aids for the presentation you planned, such as videos, props or alternative presentation software and apps. You could also conduct research into how inventors, designers and businesses present and explain their innovations and inventions to the public.

Chapter 3 Arguing and persuading
Extreme sports

What's it all about?

This chapter develops the skills needed to write persuasively.
It looks at a range of texts on the theme of extreme sports, and
explores the techniques that writers use to convince their readers
or audiences of their point of view. You will read texts from
websites and feature articles, and will take part in a formal debate.

You should already know:

- how to distinguish between fact and opinion in texts
- how to identify the purpose of a text
- how to use quotations to support your ideas
- how to comment on a writer's word choices
- how to use complex sentences to develop your ideas
- that writers use techniques to make their writing persuasive
- how to plan and deliver a persuasive speech in a familiar context.

You will learn how to:

- identify persuasive techniques and comment on them
- identify and comment on viewpoint and bias in a text
- comment on how a text has been organised
- plan and deliver a persuasive speech as part of a formal debate
- vary sentence lengths and structures for effect
- structure a persuasive text effectively.

You will:

- take part in a formal debate about banning extreme sports
- write a persuasive letter to a friend, encouraging them to take up a sport
- comment on and respond to a text about extreme sports.

Enjoy reading

You will learn how to:
- share your first impressions of an opinion article
- work out what it is about and why it has been written.

You are going to read an extract from an article called 'Why you should let your kids do extreme sports'.

1 Think about the title of the article.

a) What are extreme sports?

b) Can you think of any examples of extreme sports?

c) Can you think of any reasons why doing extreme sports might be good for children?

2 Read the extract slowly, noting down any words you do not know.

Why you should let your kids do extreme sports

Experts say intense outdoor activities can help children increase focus and develop a better awareness of their surroundings

Walk around the base of any downhill-mountain-bike park, and the people [pedalling] look like extras from the movie *Batman*: full-face helmets, body [armour], and bikes that could withstand a typhoon. They throw themselves off steep drops and bomb down narrow trails. The totality of downhill mountain biking—the uniform, the speed, the daring— entranced my two sons, eight-year-old Henry and six-year- old Silas, this summer. We spend a lot of time in Colorado's Winter Park, and the resort's Trestle Bike Park is always abuzz with downhillers. Over and over the kids begged to try it. Our regular old bike rides, the kind where you have to pedal uphill instead of taking a chairlift, the kind where you wear shorts and a shirt instead of a back protector and full-face helmet, were now apparently too tame for Henry and Silas.

I thought otherwise. It wasn't the potential physical danger that gave me pause. I simply questioned the wisdom of exposing young kids to extreme sports. I couldn't **see the smarts** in taking a formative childhood pastime like bike riding and making it into a gear-intensive, expensive, adult(ish) thing.

[...]

But most of all, I just couldn't shake the cynical suspicion 25 that extreme sports for kids—there's youth kitesurfing, rock climbing, freeride skiing, spearfishing, and Spartan Races, to name a few—were developed entirely to manipulate **Gen-X** and **Millennial** parents' **Peter Pan syndrome**, so we'd crack open our wallets and pay for lessons and gear. *Lessons?* When 30 I learned how to ride a bike, there were no lessons—unless you count face-planting on the asphalt, my banana-seat **Schwinn** overturned beside me, as a sort of clinic.

Meanwhile, the boys relentlessly repeated their argument: downhill mountain biking looked fun, and they wanted to 35 try it.

I reached out to Richard Louv, journalist and author of *Vitamin N, The Essential Guide to a Nature-Rich Life*, who **spawned the term** 'nature-deficit disorder'. Specifically, he believes that kids should spend a lot more unstructured time in nature so that 40 they develop into curious, capable humans. Surely he would think downhill mountain biking, or any extreme sport for that matter, didn't count as quality nature time for kids, since there's a lot of structure and stuff involved. To my surprise, Louv said he was 'fine with the Millennial or Gen-X approach 45 to extreme outdoor sports, with a few words of caution.' Specifically, Louv said that the best nature experiences for young children are those that are personal, tactile, and slow, like getting muddy, climbing a tree, or watching fish jumping for flies at a lake. Although extreme sports aren't slow, he 50 said, they can be personal and extremely stimulating. 'Young people are more likely to be attracted to riskier outdoor adventures,' he said. They can still commune with nature, even if they're going fast and are wearing body [armour]. In fact, the risk inherent in extreme sports might make some 55 kids 'more aware of their surroundings,' Louv said.

That increased awareness could well spread to other aspects of their lives, like school and home. This is a good thing, according to Angela Hanscom [...] founder of TimberNook, a nature-based kids camp. 'One of the most significant 60 impacts of nature-deficit disorder is a decrease in attention span,' she said. This inattention has been linked to a lack of movement. Kids who are sedentary and staring at screens are not stimulating their balance or organizing their senses, she said. 'Those kids tend to have trouble controlling emotions, 65 are more easily frustrated, and struggle with hyperactivity,' Hanscom added.

Vocabulary

see the smarts: see the sense or reason in something

Gen-X: Generation X, the generation born from the early 1960s to late 1970s

Millennial: a person who was born in the 1980s and 1990s and reached young adulthood in the early twenty-first century

Peter Pan syndrome: an inability to grow up or engage in adult behaviour

Schwinn: a brand of popular bicycle

spawned the term: created the expression or name

Time spent playing in nature helps young kids develop their neurological systems, and they inherently seek out the stimulation they need. For instance, when kids spin until 70 they're dizzy and fall down, that helps them organize their senses and develop their balance and brains.

Time in nature also helps kids navigate fear, and extreme sports might provide even more opportunities for that than, say, a nature walk. 'When kids are able to try things that 75 scare them, and realize they can overcome the challenges, that's very important for their development,' Hanscom said.

From www.outsideonline.com by Rachel Walker

3 Now choose five of the words you noted down. Can you work out what each one means?

   a) What sort of word is it: a verb, adjective, adverb or noun?

   b) Does it contain a prefix or suffix you know already? (For example, 'im' is a prefix meaning 'not'.)

   c) Does the context help? Look at the rest of the sentence – what is happening?

4 Note down answers to the following big five questions.

   a) Who is this article about?

   b) What issue is discussed in the article?

   c) When are the events happening: now or in the past or the future?

   d) Where do the events take place?

   e) Why has the writer written this text?

5 What did you like or find interesting about this article?

6 This extract is from a type of writing called an opinion article. This is a piece of writing, usually published in a newspaper or magazine, in which a writer argues their point of view about a current topic or issue. Can you find a phrase or sentence which shows that this is an opinion article?

7 Have you ever read anything like this before? Is it the kind of writing you normally read? Why? Why not?

8 Did this extract make you want to read on? Why? Why not?

9 What do you think about the writer's viewpoint in this article? Do you agree? Why? Why not?

What is writing to argue and persuade?

You will learn how to:
- identify features of different types of persuasive texts
- comment on the use of positive language choices to persuade readers or to present a point of view.

Texts that have a clear point of view are sometimes called *persuasive* texts or *argumentative* texts. Writers choose their language carefully to build up a convincing point of view or argument.

Explore

Persuasive texts aim to convince the reader of something, whether it is to do or buy something or to convince them of a point of view.

There are many different types of persuasive texts, including promotional leaflets or websites, speeches and advertisements. Adverts are persuasive texts that are used to sell a product or service. **Feature articles** are actually types of **argument writing** and will consider different arguments or ideas before coming to a conclusion about an issue.

Read the following extract.

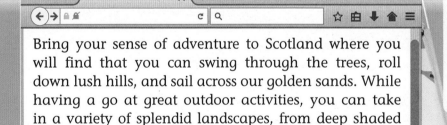

Bring your sense of adventure to Scotland where you will find that you can swing through the trees, roll down lush hills, and sail across our golden sands. While having a go at great outdoor activities, you can take in a variety of splendid landscapes, from deep shaded forests to stunning coastlines.

From www.visitscotland.com

Key terms

feature article: an article in a newspaper or magazine that deals with a topic in depth

argument writing: a type of text that argues for a point of view, through considering and dismissing different ideas, before coming to a conclusion

1 What sort of text is this and what do you think it wants to persuade its readers to do?

Notice how the text:

- only includes the best aspects of Scotland to make it sound attractive to potential tourists

- uses positive vocabulary to make the place sound beautiful

- addresses the reader directly (using the **pronoun** 'you') to add a personal touch.

Key term

pronoun: a word used instead of a noun, such as 'he', 'she', 'it', 'they', 'we', 'I', 'you'

2 What are the connotations of the following positive word choices? Write the words down, then make notes about what they suggest about Scotland. For example:

golden: This suggests that the sands are shining and precious.

a) lush

b) great

c) splendid

d) deep

e) stunning

As persuasive texts often present only one view, they can be considered **biased**.

Texts that argue for a particular point of view, such as the following feature article on extreme sports, may consider several opinions. However, they will often lean towards one, by using evidence and support from experts to make this point of view seem stronger.

Key term

biased: showing favour towards one side of an argument more than another; showing favour for or against someone or something

Read the following extract from Rachel Walker's feature article about extreme sports.

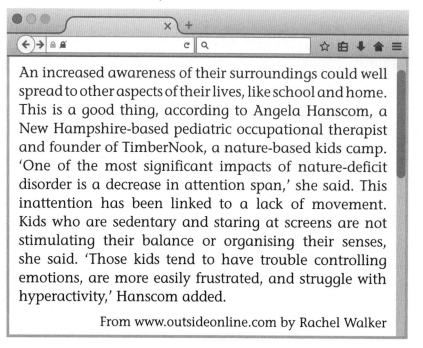

An increased awareness of their surroundings could well spread to other aspects of their lives, like school and home. This is a good thing, according to Angela Hanscom, a New Hampshire-based pediatric occupational therapist and founder of TimberNook, a nature-based kids camp. 'One of the most significant impacts of nature-deficit disorder is a decrease in attention span,' she said. This inattention has been linked to a lack of movement. Kids who are sedentary and staring at screens are not stimulating their balance or organising their senses, she said. 'Those kids tend to have trouble controlling emotions, are more easily frustrated, and struggle with hyperactivity,' Hanscom added.

From www.outsideonline.com by Rachel Walker

3 What **viewpoint** does the writer express here? Explain why you think this.

4 How do the quotations from Angela Hanscom help to support this viewpoint?

5 Could this text be viewed as biased? Why?

Develop

6 Look at the following extracts from texts that are persuasive or express a point of view. Which ones use **direct address**?

   a) 'In North America, you will find our road trips take you to the best national parks for hiking heaven.'

   b) 'Kids who are sedentary and staring at screens are not stimulating their balance or organising their senses.'

   c) 'If you think that ride-on mowers can't offer much of a spectacle, think again!'

7 Which type of text do you think each of the extracts above come from? How can you tell?

Key term
....
viewpoint: the attitude or feelings a writer or character has towards people or events

Key term
....
direct address: the use of the pronoun 'you' in a text to make the reader feel as if the writer is addressing them personally

Now read the following extract from a feature article about cycling holidays.

> Cycling holidays are simply the best. By getting out of your car and onto a bike you are able to access the hidden corners of destinations, discover remote villages and meet the friendly locals. Recently I cycled along the stunning coastline in Sardinia. Not only was I able to appreciate the beautiful vista, but I felt myself becoming fitter and healthier too!

8 Find examples of the following features in the extract above:

   a) positive adjectives

   b) direct address

   c) the **rule of three**.

9 Write a short paragraph explaining how the writer makes the cycling holidays sound appealing.

You can use the following starter:

> The writer persuades us to consider a cycling holiday by...

Key term

rule of three: a useful pattern of three examples, which makes the information or idea expressed memorable

Respond

10 a) Look back at the extract from the article about extreme sports. Which of the techniques listed in Question 8 does the writer use and not use? Why do you think this is the case?

   b) Which other techniques are used to present the writer's point of view?

11 Write a short paragraph to show some of the ways the writer's point of view is suggested in the extract.

Exploring how persuasive and argument texts are organised

You will learn how to:
- comment on the way a text has been organised
- identify the topic sentences in a text.

Think about reading a text as making a journey. When travelling somewhere new, a good road layout, clear directions and signposts will help you reach your destination. You need the same guidance in a text: a clear structure and layout, with directions and signposts. This enables the reader to follow the argument.

Explore

Read the following extract from a text about base jumper Jeb Corliss.

Jeb Corliss

Over his short illustrious career, **base jumper** Jeb Corliss has completed over 2,000 stunts including leaping off France's Eiffel Tower, zooming through a waterfall in the Swiss Alps and even, flying across the Tianmen Cave, a 100ft-wide water eroded slit, in China's Tianmen Mountain. However, the stunt he pulled recently was so dangerous that it scared the daredevil himself. This time around the 'flying dagger' as he is now being called, decided to take on a tiny fissure between the two peaks of the 2,677 feet tall Mount Jianglang in China. Measuring about […] the size of three football fields, the peaks twist and curve in such a way that at about the halfway point, there is just a [7.6 metre] wide gap between the two. While this may not be a big deal in a jet-propelled flight, given that Jeb propels on his own might using just the **wingsuit**, even a slight wind **turbulence** could easily derail his path and result in a crash landing.

From www.dogonews.com

Vocabulary

base jumper: someone who jumps from a fixed object, using a parachute to descend safely, for sport

wingsuit: a one-piece outfit with sections of fabric between the arms and legs that allow someone to glide when in freefall

turbulence: a violent or unsteady movement of air

1 The text doesn't have paragraphs. How does this affect how easy it is to read?

2 Which of the following statements are true about this text?

a) It includes subheadings.

b) It uses presentational devices such as pictures and captions.

c) It contains connectives, such as 'and', 'because' and 'however', to signal the direction of the argument.

Writers begin a new paragraph when they start writing about a new time, person, topic or place.

3 How many paragraphs should the article be split into? Where should each paragraph begin? Write down the reason for your choices.

> **Develop**

One structural feature of paragraphs is the **topic sentence**, which introduces the main focus of the paragraph. This is considered the most important sentence in a paragraph and is usually the opening sentence.

4 Identify and note down the topic sentences in each of the paragraphs decided on in Question 3.

Subheadings briefly tell the reader what is in each section of a text. Writers still use a topic sentence to introduce the paragraph beneath each subheading. For example, the subheadings for the two paragraphs of the article here could be 'Background to Jeb Corliss' and 'The latest challenge'.

Key term

topic sentence: a sentence in a paragraph – usually at the beginning – that shows the reader the main subject of the writing

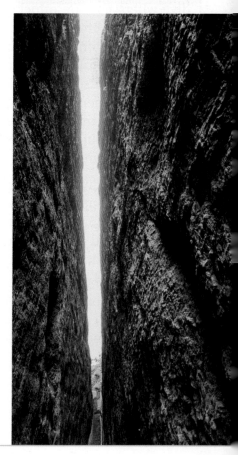

Respond

Read the following text about skydiving and parachuting.

Skydiving & Parachuting

Throwing yourself out of a perfectly good plane may sound like a crazy plan, but skydiving in Northern Ireland is a must-try for adventurists. Jump out of an aircraft, and freefall (skydiving) before returning to earth with the aid of a parachute. As you fall through the sky you will be rewarded with breathtaking views – if you can keep your eyes open that is.

A good way to get started is to get in contact with a centre that specialises in skydiving and parachuting. This is a cost effective way to see if the sport is for you. It's advisable to find one that operates under the regulations of the British Parachute Association. Also, centres generally have restrictions for safety reasons, for example, you need to be 16 years old to jump.

The most popular jump for beginners is a tandem sky-dive where you are attached to an instructor. You only need a short briefing for this one and the freefall lasts for about a minute. If you enjoy the tandem skydive and want to take it further, the next step is to do a static-line course: a one day course where you learn about equipment, steering, and how to land. There is a progression training system which will take you from static line through to freeflow until you are classed as an experienced jumper.

A tandem skydive costs approximately £260. A static line course costs approximately £210 and each subsequent jump costs £35. Once people become very experienced and dedicated to the sport, they often consider the option of buying their own parachute, but until then, the centre will provide you with all the equipment you need.

Please note a compulsory insurance payment to the British Parachute Association of £35 is also required.

From www.discovernorthernireland.com

5 Copy the grid below and write down the topic sentences from each paragraph. Then think of a suitable subheading for each paragraph and write it in the last column.

Paragraph	Topic sentence	Subheading
1	'Throwing yourself out of a perfectly good plane may sound like a crazy plan, but skydiving in Northern Ireland is a must-try for adventurists.'	Why should you skydive?
2		
3		
4		

6 Write a sentence for each of your subheadings to explain how it helps the reader understand what is included in that section of the 'Skydiving & Parachuting' text. For example:

> I chose 'Why should you skydive?' as my subheading because the first paragraph makes skydiving sound attractive to the reader by calling it 'a must-try' and gives good reasons for doing it, such as 'breathtaking views'.

Checklist for success

✔ Look carefully for each topic sentence – remember, it is not always the first sentence in a paragraph.

✔ Make sure your subheadings reflect the content of the paragraph.

Identifying main ideas and viewpoints

You will learn how to:
- identify main points in a paragraph
- identify how facts and opinions are used to support a main point
- comment on a writer's views in a text.

Writers choose language and pictures carefully to make their opinion clear. They also often support their views with facts to make their argument more convincing or to persuade the reader to share their point of view. You need to be able to identify how writers use fact and opinion in a text in order to explain a writer's views or bias.

Explore

Read the text below from the Honda Racing Corporation website about the Dakar Rally.

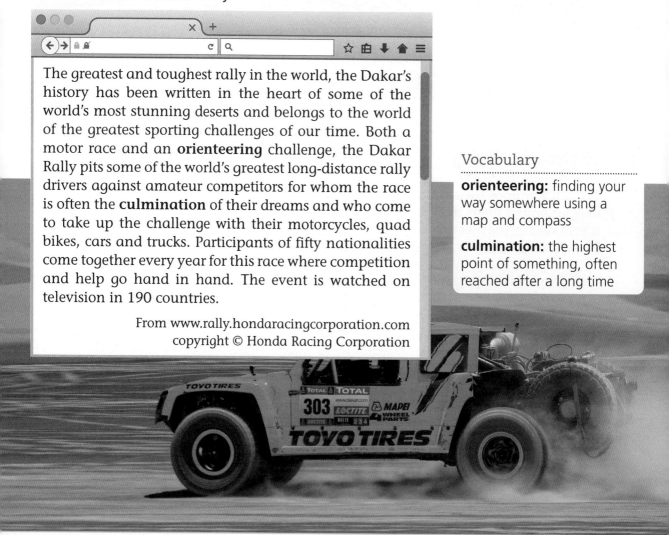

The greatest and toughest rally in the world, the Dakar's history has been written in the heart of some of the world's most stunning deserts and belongs to the world of the greatest sporting challenges of our time. Both a motor race and an **orienteering** challenge, the Dakar Rally pits some of the world's greatest long-distance rally drivers against amateur competitors for whom the race is often the **culmination** of their dreams and who come to take up the challenge with their motorcycles, quad bikes, cars and trucks. Participants of fifty nationalities come together every year for this race where competition and help go hand in hand. The event is watched on television in 190 countries.

From www.rally.hondaracingcorporation.com
copyright © Honda Racing Corporation

Vocabulary

orienteering: finding your way somewhere using a map and compass

culmination: the highest point of something, often reached after a long time

1 Using a copy of this extract, highlight the paragraph's main point.

2 Underline three additional pieces of information that the writer uses to support this main point.

In order to sound convincing, writers need to develop their ideas carefully. They can do this by introducing a main point, then using a combination of evidence, facts and persuasive opinions to support the main point. For example:

The writer makes the main point in the topic sentence: *Dakar is the greatest and toughest rally in the world.*

Supporting evidence for 'greatest': *Watched on TV in 190 countries, lots of people love to compete, amateurs and professional rally drivers.*

Supporting evidence for 'toughest': *Both a motor race and an orienteering challenge; you compete against the world's greatest long-distance rally drivers.*

3 The following statements support the main idea that Dakar is the greatest and toughest rally in the world. Identify which are facts and which are opinions.

a) 'the world's most stunning deserts'

b) 'take up the challenge with their motorcycles, quad bikes, cars and trucks'

c) 'Participants of fifty nationalities come together every year'

d) 'The event is watched on television in 190 countries'

e) 'belongs to the world of the greatest sporting challenges of our time'.

4 Add notes to explain how each of the statements above helps to make the main point sound convincing. For example:

'the world's most stunning deserts' = opinion. The word 'stunning' makes the rally sound great, as it takes place in what the writer believes is a dramatically beautiful place.

5 Writers also use **statistics** to make their point of view convincing. Which of the statements in Question 3 use statistics?

Key term

statistics: numbers such as percentages, often used as facts to support a point

6 Does the writer show bias in this description of the Dakar Rally? Write a paragraph explaining the view of the writer and how it is supported with fact and opinion. You should also comment on the writer's choice of words, giving examples.

Develop

Read the following extract about the British 12-Hour Lawnmower Race.

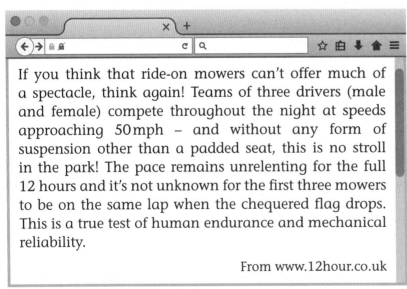

If you think that ride-on mowers can't offer much of a spectacle, think again! Teams of three drivers (male and female) compete throughout the night at speeds approaching 50 mph – and without any form of suspension other than a padded seat, this is no stroll in the park! The pace remains unrelenting for the full 12 hours and it's not unknown for the first three mowers to be on the same lap when the chequered flag drops. This is a true test of human endurance and mechanical reliability.

From www.12hour.co.uk

7 Look carefully at the topic sentence. Write down the main point of this paragraph in your own words.

8 The writer expresses a viewpoint by combining opinion with facts. Identify which of these quotations from the extract are fact and which are opinion.

   a) 'Teams of three drivers [...] compete throughout the night at speeds approaching 50 mph'

   b) 'this is no stroll in the park!'

   c) 'without any form of suspension other than a padded seat'

   d) 'This is a true test of human endurance and mechanical reliability.'

9 The writer's viewpoint or bias is also expressed through language choices. Identify words or phrases that reveal the writer's views and make a note explaining why.

Respond

10 Write a paragraph explaining how the writer develops their views about the 12-Hour Lawnmower Race. Use the following sentence starters:

> The writer begins the paragraph with a topic sentence that says that ride-on lawnmowers…
>
> For example, '…'
>
> This idea is developed when…
>
> This supports the main idea because…
>
> It is further developed when…
>
> This makes the writer's view sound convincing because…

Checklist for success

✔ Identify the writer's opinion.

✔ Include relevant quotations.

✔ Identify supporting evidence.

✔ Summarise how bias is or is not shown.

Reviewing persuasive techniques

You will learn how to:
- identify persuasive techniques
- comment on the tone of a text.

Explore

Adverts – whether they are on posters, on television, in the form of leaflets or websites – are persuasive texts because they are trying to sell you a product or service.

Read the following extract from a text about extreme climbing.

> Have you ever wondered what it would be like to scale one of the world's largest mountains? Imagine climbing above the earth's atmosphere, experiencing the thrill of adrenaline, and then gazing back down at the natural wonder you have conquered. Well, now that opportunity can be yours.

You can use the acronym AFOREST to help you remember the persuasive techniques that writers use.

A = Adjectives
F = Facts
O = Opinions
R = Rule of three
E = Emotive language
S = Statistics
T = Talk to the reader (personal pronouns)

1 Which persuasive techniques are used in this text?

Develop

Read the following extract from an article about the risks of mountaineering.

> The numbers of climbers risking their lives, as they attempt to scale and descend the world's biggest mountains, are increasing. At least six climbers have died this year alone, trying to conquer Mount Everest. Hundreds of mountaineers have waited in oxygen-draining tailbacks beneath the summit, risking frostbite and altitude sickness in order to reach the top. Clearly this has got to stop. In a time when anyone can pay $10,000 to climb this deadly peak, we need to consider if human life is now valued less than the achievement of a personal ambition.

2   Look again at the list of persuasive techniques. Which ones are used in this text? Are they the same as the ones that were used in the first text?

3   What effect does this choice of persuasive techniques have? Choose from one of the following responses.

   a) It is more direct and bossy.

   b) It is more thoughtful and logical.

   c) It is more personal and emotive.

   d) It is more distant and impartial.

The overall tone of a text should suit its audience and purpose. The tone may reflect a particular point of view or it may be neutral. It might be emotional, serious or humorous.

4   Choose five words from the second extract that you think help create its tone.

Respond

5   Reread the second extract. Identify three persuasive techniques and write a paragraph explaining the effect created by each one.

Checklist for success

✔ Identify a range of persuasive techniques.

✔ Think about the effect these techniques have on you as a reader.

✔ Comment on the tone of the writing.

Preparing a formal debate

You will learn how to:
- take part in a formal debate.

A debate is an organised argument. Debates are a good way to discuss your ideas and find out what other people think about a topic.

Explore

1. Do you think extreme sports, such as snowboarding, kitesurfing and base jumping, should be banned? Work in pairs. Without any preparation, take it in turns to try to convince your partner of your point of view. When you have finished speaking, allow your partner to question you on your opinion.

2. Discuss with your partner how convincing you thought their argument was, and vice versa. Give your reasons. Think about whether they provided evidence and examples to support their points and whether they were able to answer your questions confidently.

You are going to prepare a formal group debate. Look at these guidelines:

- Choose a 'motion' (the topic you will be debating) – for example, 'We believe that city centres should be car-free at least one day every week'.

- Form two teams of three: the proposition team (for the motion) and the opposition team (against the motion).

- Allocate roles for each team member: captain, seconder and the third team member.

- The proposition team captain begins by putting forward an overview of their point of view.

- The opposition team captain goes next, putting forward an overview of the opposing point of view.

- The seconders speak after both captains have spoken. The seconder **rebuts** the opposition captain's arguments, then makes two or three more arguments for their team.

- The third speaker on each team sums up the team's main argument in a closing statement.

Key term

rebut: to claim or prove that an argument or evidence is wrong

3 First, you need to prepare your arguments. Read the arguments against extreme sports in the grid below. Copy the grid and add three more points to the list. Add examples in the 'Evidence' column.

Against	Evidence
risk of injury	
can get into trouble from the law if using public spaces	

4 You will also need to consider ideas that the opposing team may put forward so you can prepare to argue against them. Copy the following grid. Add to the ideas in the first column, then complete the second column.

For	This argument is not strong because...
adrenaline rush	
intense workout	

When you are listening to the opposing team talking, you should add to your planning notes. You could:

- tick the points on your planning grid that they have made
- write a list of any additional key points they make
- number the points they make
- annotate your list/grid with specific phrases, facts and statistics they mention
- highlight sections of your grid that will help you to make a reasoned response to their arguments.

When you respond to the opposing team, you could:

- respond to their points in order, e.g. 'Firstly you claimed that…'
- refer to specific words, phrases, facts or statistics they mentioned which you think are questionable, e.g. 'When you said it is "essential", this is clearly not the case.'
- explain how and why these details are questionable, e.g. 'This is because…'
- Make links to your research and evidence to further support your argument, e.g. 'Furthermore, I know for a fact that…'.

Develop

A good debate team will:

- use facts and statistics as evidence
- use opinion to persuade others to agree
- listen to the other team and comment on what they have said
- structure each point using the format: state, explain, illustrate (give examples/evidence).

5 Imagine that you are the proposing team in a debate for the motion, 'Extreme sports are dangerous and should be banned'. Read the opposer's statement in the speech bubble below and make notes about what they say and the weaknesses in their argument.

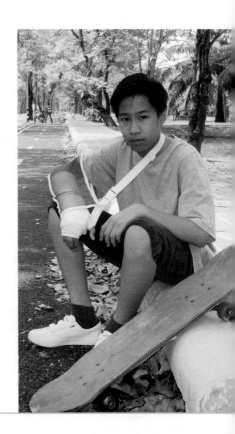

Recent research has proven that you are more likely to be injured playing football or basketball than when you are surfing or mountain biking. So, if we are to say that extreme sports need to be banned because of the risk involved, then we would also need to ban these more traditional sports. We can't do that, because we all need to stay fit and well. Therefore, extreme sports are necessary for keeping young people healthy.

6   Now write your response to the opposer's statement.

Respond

7   In groups of six, take part in a debate on the motion, 'Extreme sports are dangerous and should be banned'. Follow the rules above and choose a 'judge' to decide which team makes the most convincing argument.

8   Now, evaluate your contribution to the debate by answering the following questions.

a)   Did you explain your views clearly to the other team? How did you do this?

b)   Did you support your ideas with evidence? How successful were you in doing this? Why?

c)   Did you listen carefully to the opposing team and respond successfully to their views? How did you do this?

d)   What were your overall strengths and areas for improvement?

Using phrases to develop persuasive sentences

You will learn how to:
- use different sentence structures
- vary your sentence lengths and structures for effect.

Different sentence structures can have different effects on a reader. Writers choose their sentence structures and lengths carefully to expand on their points or make their argument more convincing.

Explore

1   Read the following sentences. What is different about each one?

   a) Why not have a go at archery, paintballing or quad biking?

   b) Sphering is an exhilarating activity.

   c) It is the perfect activity for those who love adventure!

   d) Feel the sea breeze on your face as you sail in an elegant yacht.

Each sentence has a different function:

- *Declarative sentences* make a statement.

- *Interrogative sentences* ask a question or make a request.

- *Imperative sentences* give a command.

- *Exclamatory sentences* make an exclamation.

2   Which of the sentences in Question 1 do you think engages the reader the most? Why?

Read this extract from the Travel Impressions holiday website.

> Asia not only has something for everyone, but a lot of it! (a) Looking for history? (b) The region's history dates back 5,000 years. (c) Natural landscapes? (d) <u>Find mountains, deserts, rock pillars and limestone karsts as well as incredible wildlife.</u> (e) More of a city slicker? (f) The big cities are bustling metropolises with dynamic energy (g). Interested in sacred spaces and cultural immersion? (h) Discover ancient temples, holy shrines and unique religions. (i)
>
> Your Tailor-Made tour can be as long or as short as you wish, include as much or as little as you want and can range from iconic attractions to roads less travelled (j) – all with your private Local Guides adding a distinct perspective. (k)
>
> Because travel is not just a journey. It's an experience. (l)
>
> From www.travimp.com

3 Match each sentence a–l with a sentence function. For example:

> *e = imperative sentence*

4 How do the declarative sentences help the reader understand the topic better?

5 How many imperative sentences are there? How does this type of sentence involve the reader?

6 There are several questions in this extract. Who are they addressed to? Why is this sentence function a persuasive technique?

When you are writing persuasively, it is important to make the reader feel involved in your message. By asking questions and giving commands you make the reader feel you are addressing them personally.

Rhetorical questions are often used in persuasive texts to get the reader thinking about something and to make them feel involved. For example: 'Do you want to experience the holiday of a lifetime?'

Imperative sentences are persuasive because they begin with a verb, inviting the reader/listener to *do* something.

Key term
....
rhetorical question: a question that is used to make people think, rather than requiring an answer

7 Copy and complete the following imperative sentences and rhetorical questions with your own sentence endings about an interesting or beautiful place you know.

   a) Do you want to...?

   b) Fancy a...?

   c) Take a...

Develop

When writing persuasively, it is important to convince your reader that you know about your subject.

Read this text about mountain biking. What do you notice about the beginning of each sentence?

> During your visit, you will have the opportunity to experience a variety of stunning routes, from the rugged mountains to gnarly forest trails. Beneath the forest canopy, you will find the high-speed single track – a challenge for our most adventurous mountain bikers.

Each sentence begins with a **preposition**. Prepositions help the reader to work out the location of something in time or place. These are some common prepositions:

> about above among below beneath
> across during by in through until

8 Think of three more prepositions.

Prepositional phrases are used to help answer the key questions of *where, when, how, what, which* and *whose*. Using prepositional phrases in your writing helps you to sound more convincing because it adds more detail to what you are saying. This makes you sound more authoritative.

Key terms

preposition: a word that goes before a noun to describe its relationship to another thing or person ('*on* the table', '*by* my bed')

prepositional phrase: a group of words that begins with a preposition and ends with a noun or pronoun ('above the track', 'over the lake')

9   Look back at the short text on mountain biking. Which question of where, when, how, what, which and whose, does the prepositional phrase in each sentence help you to answer?

10   Rewrite the following sentences by adding a prepositional phrase to the beginning.

   a)   You can try free-diving.

   b)   You will find a range of activities to take part in.

> **Respond**

11   Write a paragraph for a tourist website, persuading visitors to get involved in outdoor activities in your area.

Checklist for success

✔ Use imperative sentences to command the reader.

✔ Use rhetorical questions to make the reader think.

✔ Use declaratives to add facts and information.

✔ Use exclamatory sentences to make the activities sound exciting.

✔ Use prepositional phrases to add detail.

Structuring an effective persuasive text

You will learn how to:
- structure a persuasive text effectively
- lay out a persuasive text appropriately.

A persuasive text needs to be structured carefully to convince your reader.

Explore

Read the following extract from a travel website.

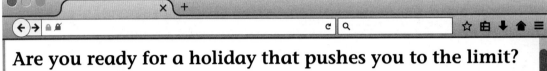

Are you ready for a holiday that pushes you to the limit?

Explore the world from a kayak, a mountain bike or by rope! Our adrenaline-packed experiences are not for the faint-hearted. Whether you are a first-timer or an experienced adventurer, then *X-treme Holidays* has a package for you.

Tailor-made holidays

Imagine kayaking through white-water rapids in the Himalayas, climbing colossal canyons in Oman and biking downhill in Peru. Our *X-treme Holidays* have something for everyone. If you are looking for a shorter holiday or weekend break, then try one of our 3-day adrenaline experiences, for example an adventure package in South Africa including abseiling, diving with sharks and bungee jumping. Or if you have a longer time to explore, then spend a week hiking in the legendary Himalayas.

Specialist support

Our expert and passionate local guides will show you around, give you lots of tips, and provide a true insight into the local way of life. All our *X-treme Holidays* are also fully supported by a team of specialist professionals, who will guide you through your nail-biting adventures.

Satisfaction guaranteed

X-treme holidays: guaranteed to make your heart pound and push you to your limits!

Our accreditations

10 reviews ✓✓✓✓✓ 100%

Gold Service Award
★★★★★

Thrill rating

1. Look at the first heading. How does it grab the reader's attention? Think about the use of language and presentation.

2. Look carefully at the first paragraph. What does it promise the reader? Why do you think this is important?

3. How does paragraph 2 appeal to the reader's imagination?

4. What information does paragraph 3 add?

5. How does the writer make the reader feel at the end of the text? What techniques does the writer use to achieve this effect?

6. How does the writer use the four headings?

7. How do the images used make the holidays seem attractive?

8. Why does the webpage include an accreditation and rating feature? Comment on how they attract the reader's attention.

A popular way of structuring a persuasive text is to use the four Ps:

- **Promise:** tell the reader what they will gain.
- **Picture:** fill out the promise using vibrant, descriptive language; ask the reader to imagine themselves enjoying the benefits of the object/activity/offer.
- **Proof:** add facts and statistics.
- **Push:** guarantee the reader that they will benefit from the object/activity/offer.

9   Match each of the following sentences to one of the four Ps.

   a) 'Imagine kayaking through white-water rapids in the Himalayas, climbing colossal canyons in Oman and biking downhill in Peru.'

   b) 'All our *X-treme Holidays* are also fully supported by a team of specialist professionals, who will guide you through your nail-biting adventures.'

   c) 'Whether you are a first-timer or experienced adventurer, then *X-treme Holidays* has a package for you.'

   d) '*X-treme holidays* – guaranteed to make your heart pound and push you to your limits.'

Develop

10 Choose an activity or sport that you know something about. You are going to plan a short internet article to promote it. Copy the following grid and make notes about your sport/activity.

Name of chosen sport/activity:		
What it involves	Benefits of the sport/activity	Evidence (research/facts/ statistics)

11 Next, decide how you will encourage people to get involved. Copy and complete the grid below to plan the ideas, structure and layout for your writing.

The four Ps	
Promise: What is in it for them?	
Picture: Fill out the promise. Ask the reader to imagine being involved. Use descriptive language.	
Proof: Use evidence to back up the benefits, e.g. facts, statistics, research, testimonials.	
Push: A final guarantee that they will enjoy this sport.	
Attention grabbing headings	
Engaging photos/images	

Think carefully about how you could present your article to attract readers' attention.

What type of images of photographs would be effective? For example:

- photographs of people taking part in the sport/activity or of the location
- photographs that make the activity seem challenging or fun
- a close-up of one person or a medium shot of a group of people.

How big do you want the images to be? Should they have equal importance to the text, or do you want to keep the text as the main focus?

How should you lay out your article? You could consider:

- an attention-grabbing headline, with subheadings for each paragraph

- a one-column layout, with the article and headings in one column, and menus along the side

- a featured image layout, which uses a large image as a focal point

- the use of multiple smaller images, placed around the text.

Create a rough sketch of how you want to lay out and present your article, as part of your plan.

12 In order to link your ideas in each paragraph, you can use connectives – for example 'Furthermore, 'However' and 'As a result of'. This will make your text flow better and sound more convincing by showing a causal link between points or by adding evidence to what you have written.

Match the connectives to the function.

Connective	Function
as a result of	opposition
furthermore	indicating result
however	addition

13 Now choose a connective that you will use in each section of your 4Ps to link ideas between (or within) your paragraphs. Add it to your planning grid.

Key term

connective: a linking word or phrase used in a sentence (e.g. 'and', 'but', 'or', 'so', 'then', 'because', 'after')

Respond

14 Now, using your plan, write your short internet article promoting a new sports or activity club.

Checklist for success

✔ Explain what the sport involves.

✔ Clearly outline how the reader will benefit from it.

✔ Use descriptive language to help the reader picture themselves taking part.

✔ Provide evidence to support your points.

✔ Lay out your webpage appropriately, and choose engaging images.

✔ End with a memorable final line to push your point.

Writing your own persuasive letter

You will learn how to:
- combine the persuasive and argumentative writing skills you have learned in one text
- understand what makes a high-level piece of persuasive writing.

Your task

Write a letter encouraging students from your school to go on a school trip that includes sporting activities. You should include:

- why they should come on the school trip with you

- details about the school trip

- evidence about the quality of the trip

- your guarantee that they will have a good time.

Approaching the task

1 Plan your ideas. Your plan could take the form of a spider diagram. For example:

great reviews from students who have been on trip before

beautiful views

hiking holiday

chance to see the world with your friends

visit Atlas Mountains in Morocco

2 Choose your best ideas and decide which order you will put them in. For example:

Paragraph	Focus on
1	Promise an exciting hiking trip which will improve our fitness and allow us to see beautiful places.
2	
3	
4	

3 Copy the following checklist to make sure you plan for all the different features of a persuasive text. Tick off each skill or feature as you use it in your draft.

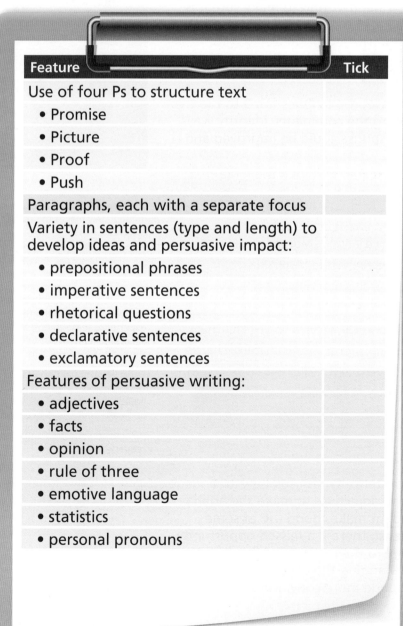

Feature	Tick
Use of four Ps to structure text	
• Promise	
• Picture	
• Proof	
• Push	
Paragraphs, each with a separate focus	
Variety in sentences (type and length) to develop ideas and persuasive impact:	
• prepositional phrases	
• imperative sentences	
• rhetorical questions	
• declarative sentences	
• exclamatory sentences	
Features of persuasive writing:	
• adjectives	
• facts	
• opinion	
• rule of three	
• emotive language	
• statistics	
• personal pronouns	

4 Come up with a striking opening sentence or two. For example:

> Come hiking with us in Morocco! We will become fitter, healthier and happier, as we climb up the stunning Atlas Mountains.

5 a) Now write your letter.

b) When you have finished, read through your work and check for any errors in spelling, punctuation and grammar. If there are any spellings that you are unsure of, look them up in a dictionary, then correct them.

c) Finally check your handwriting to make sure it is neat and legible.

Reflecting on your work

6 Compare your own response to Question 5 to the two responses below. Using the comments, identify ways in which your own response could be improved and rewrite it, if needed.

Response 1

> Dear Student,
> Come hiking with your school friends in Morocco! We will be able to trek through the amazing Atlas Mountains, camp in the wilderness and then visit the bustling city of Marrakesh.
>   During our stay, we will have the chance to see charming villages on the mountainsides, above the beautiful orchards of fruit and walnut trees. By exploring the rugged beauty of Northern Africa together, we will become healthier friends.
>   Do you want to pass up this opportunity?

The opening imperative sentence immediately makes the reader feel involved.

The rule of three and two adjectives engage the reader.

Use of a prepositional phrase at the beginning of the sentence adds specific details about when the reader will experience these things; adjectives 'charming' and 'beautiful' also make the sights sound positive.

The prepositional phrase links the ideas together and 'rugged' is an interesting adjective choice; more emotive language could have been chosen.

A rhetorical question appeals to the reader's feelings.

Comment on Response 1

There is a wide range of sentence types used here to engage the reader, and some varied adjectives to make the holiday sound appealing. The student makes good use of some persuasive features. However, there is a missed opportunity to make an emotive appeal to the reader, and 'healthier friends' is weak. Perhaps changing the vocabulary here would make the writing sound more convincing.

Response 2

Dear Fellow Students,

Have you ever felt that you are not getting enough excitement out of life? Well, come mountain biking with us in Peru!

During our trip, we will have access to extraordinary terrain, high-quality tracks and the most amazing scenery. Through exploring the extreme trails, we will be able to hone our cycling technique, whilst also having the opportunity to explore the unique history and culture of the area.

Surely you cannot want to miss out on this fantastic opportunity?

The opening rhetorical sentence immediately addresses the reader.

The use of the imperative further engages the reader and the adverb 'well' creates a friendly tone.

The list of three and positive adjectives reinforce the persuasive tone.

Use of prepositional phrase at beginning of sentence adds specific details about when the reader will experience these things; adjectives 'extreme' and 'unique' also make the experience sound unmissable.

A rhetorical question and the intensifier 'surely' appeals to the reader's sense that they need to take part.

Comment on Response 2

There is a wider range of connectives used here to link sentences and engage the reader, and some more precise use of adjectives to make the holiday sound unmissable. The student makes very effective use of some persuasive features. Perhaps more specific examples of the benefits of the trip would help to further persuade the reader.

Responding to an argument text

You will learn how to:
- combine the reading skills you have learned when responding to a persuasive text
- understand what makes a high-level response to persuasive writing.

You are going to explore the ways in which the text you read at the start of this chapter works, using the understanding you have built up in this chapter.

Understanding the text

1. Write a sentence in response to each of the following questions.

   a) What is the main subject or topic of this text?

   b) What is the viewpoint or information the writer wants to get across?

   c) Why do they want to make this point or convey this information?

   d) Who is the writer and who is the audience or reader?

   e) What form is the text written in? How do you know?

Thinking about the text's purpose and features

2 Look again at the extract. Which features of persuasion can you identify? Copy and complete the grid with the relevant quotations or line numbers.

Persuasive feature	Quotation/line number
powerful adjectives	
rhetorical questions	
expert opinions	
evidence – through examples	
emotive language	

The text works well because of the writer's choice of vocabulary. Reread this sentence and answer the question below.

> The totality of downhill mountain biking—the uniform, the speed, the daring—entranced my two sons, eight-year-old Henry and six-year-old Silas, this summer.

3 The phrase 'totality of downhill mountain biking' creates a sense of how absorbing the sport is. Find other words or phrases that create this sense.

4 Select three words or phrases which suggest that downhill mountain biking is exciting.

5 Find two examples of sentences where additional details have been included using bracketing dashes.

6 Look at the final paragraph. Give three quotations about the benefits of quality nature time. For each quotation, explain how the language choices suggest the benefits.

- Quotation: _____
- Effect: _____
- Quotation: _____
- Effect: _____
- Quotation: _____
- Effect: _____

7 Read paragraph 2 again. How does the writer use language to make downhill mountain biking sound attractive?

> The writer presents downhill mountain biking as...
> For example, '...'
> The word/phrase '...' means...
> This word/phrase implies...
> Therefore, the writer makes the reader feel that mountain biking is...

Reflecting on your work

8 Compare your own response to Question 7 to the two responses below. Using the comments, identify ways in which your own response could be improved and rewrite it, if needed.

Response 1

The writer presents downhill mountain biking as exciting. —— Makes a clear point.

For example, 'The totality of downhill mountain biking—the —— Uses a relevant quotation.

uniform, the speed, the daring—entranced my two sons'.

The word 'totality' means that the sport takes up all of —— Explains the meanings of the word in the quotation in context.

your attention. This implies that it is a demanding and —— Explains what the word choice implies about the sport.

absorbing sport. Therefore, the writer makes the reader —— Begins to develop an explanation of the writer's views, but no reason is provided.

feel that mountain biking is challenging in a positive way.

Comment on Response 1

This answer explains the meanings of the writer's words and links these meanings to what the reader learns. However, the student needs to provide reasons for these links and focus on individual words to develop their response.

Response 2

The writer presents downhill mountain biking as extreme but exciting, when she describes 'The totality of downhill mountain biking… entranced my two sons'. The noun 'totality' means that the sport demands all of your concentration and skill, which therefore implies that it fully engages its participants. Furthermore, the use of the verb 'entranced' means that the extreme nature of downhill mountain biking is viewed as bewitching by her sons. Therefore the writer makes the reader feel that although mountain biking is challenging, it is also captivating.

Makes a clear point, using precise adjectives.

Uses short, embedded quotations.

Explains the meanings of the word in the quotation in context and uses correct subject terminology.

Explains what the word choice implies about the sport.

Unpacks a second word choice to develop explanation.

Links the writer's views to the previous explanation.

Comment on Response 2

This answer explains the explicit and implied meanings of the writer's words and links these meanings together to explain what the reader learns. However, the student could further develop their explanation of the effect on the reader.

What you have achieved

Reading

- You have identified and commented on the features of persuasive and argument writing.

- You have identified bias and commented on how it is created across a range of texts.

- You are able to understand and comment on the way writers organise texts and develop their ideas.

Writing

- You are able to vary sentence lengths and structure to create specific effects.

- You can structure a persuasive text appropriately.

- You can use the features of a persuasive text in your own writing, reflect on its effectiveness and redraft to improve your work.

Speaking and listening

- You are able to prepare for and take part in a formal debate.

- You are able to present your opinions, using evidence to explain your views.

- You are able to listen carefully to other speakers and respond to opposing arguments.

Next steps

Reading
Read a range of persuasive texts, such as feature articles, adverts and websites and work out the writer's viewpoint in each one. Keep a list of the different techniques writers use to sell their ideas to you and make notes about the effects created by each one.

Read a range of argument texts, such as feature articles and blogs. Keep a list of the different techniques writers use to build and develop ideas and make notes about the effects created by each one. Make notes on how the writers use counter-arguments.

Writing
Try writing a persuasive advert or leaflet about one of the topics you have been reading about. Alternatively, try writing an opinion article about one of the topics you've been reading about. You can choose to write from your own viewpoint, or a different viewpoint from your own.

Speaking and listening
Research a different controversial topic that you are interested in and plan a speech for a campaign. Collect information for and against this argument and use this to support your argument and second guess any counter arguments. You could film your speech, in the style of a campaign video for a charity or advert.

What's it all about?

This chapter is all about how writers present a child's view of the world. It explores the different perspectives of characters and narrators, and how these are created, and shows you how you can use a variety of approaches to viewpoint in your own stories.

You should already know:

- the key features of certain genres of story, such as mystery and suspense
- the basics of plot structure, and how to generate ideas for stories and plan your own
- that writers select from a range of techniques to create plot and characters, including direct speech
- that role-play and discussion can help you empathise with characters and explore themes.

You will learn how to:

- explore stories that present a child's view of the world and the people around them
- identify different styles of voice and viewpoint in texts with similar themes
- explain how texts can evoke different cultures or a vivid sense of place
- use discussion and role-play to bring together key ideas about stories and characters
- write short sections of stories in a range of styles, including the diary form
- plan and structure your own child-centred stories in original ways.

You will:

- take part in a role-play exploring a character from a story
- write a critical response to a story from a different culture and time
- write a key moment from a story of your own with a child as a central character.

Enjoy reading

You will learn how to:
- respond to a piece of narrative writing from a particular place and culture
- share your first impressions with a partner.

You are going to read an extract from *Follow the Rabbit-Proof Fence* by Doris Pilkington (also known as Nugi Garimara). It is about three **Aboriginal** girls who have just arrived at a **Settlement**.

1 Think about the details above and the title of the book.

   a) Who are the Aboriginal people? Do you know what country they live in?

   b) What is a 'rabbit-proof fence'? Who would build one, and why?

2 Read the extract slowly, noting down any words you do not know.

In this section, three sisters are being shown around the Settlement by other girls.

Vocabulary

Aboriginal: people who have lived in a land from the earliest known times, before the arrival of colonisers from other countries

Settlement: a place where a group of people are taken to be 're-homed'

The river and the **flats** on either side were full to overflowing. To the girls from the East Pilbara region, this chocolate-coloured river was a new and exciting spectacle, quite different from the normal pinky coloured salt lakes, creeks and rivers back home. This sight only made Molly more aware that she was a stranger in this part of the country, as were all the others in 5 this small group.

We are all cut off from our families, she thought and was overcome with a deep longing for the dry rugged, red landscape of the Pilbara. Still, sighed Molly, you couldn't help being fascinated by the swirling currents and the frothy white foam that clung to the trunks of the paperbark trees and the 10 tall river gums. As they rounded the bend of the rough road, still stepping cautiously trying to miss the muddy puddles, they were surprised to see about six or seven girls, one aged around seventeen, with a group of girls eight years old or perhaps younger, all wading across the icy cold water. The eldest girl, Edna Green, was showing the youngsters how to cross to 15 the other side by using a long stick to measure the depth of the water. The smaller girls were following their leader, their cotton shifts were tucked into their bloomers.

'Why are they doing that?' asked Rosie, who couldn't understand why anyone would go walking in the freezing river on a cold, wet day. 20

'Just for something to do, that's all,' Martha told her.

'When it's not raining we go for long walks all over the place,' said Polly.

'But you see that big rock over there,' she said, pointing across to the far side of the river. 'Well, that's a **woodarchies**' cave. Don't go over that side.'

'What are these woodarchies?' asked Rosie.   25

'Woodarchies are little hairy men. Someone saw them for real, you know, no makeup,' she said seriously.

'They must be same as **marbus**,' whispered Molly. 'This is marbu country. We can't stay here, they might kill us,' she added glancing at the grey limestone rock jutting out from behind the thick bushes.   30

From *Follow the Rabbit-Proof Fence* by Doris Pilkington/Nugi Garimara

3 Now choose five of the words you noted down. Can you work out what each one means?

a) What sort of word is it: a verb, adjective, adverb or noun?

b) Does it contain a prefix or suffix you know already? (For example, 'im' is a prefix meaning 'not'.)

c) Does the context help? Look at the rest of the sentence – what is happening?

4 Note down answers to the following big five questions.

a) **Who** is this extract about?

b) **What** is happening in the extract?

c) **When** in the story do you think this extract takes place? Why do you think this?

d) **Where** do the events take place?

e) **Why** has the writer written this text?

5 This extract is from a story that is based on real events. What evidence can you find in the extract to suggest:

a) that the events are seen through a child's **viewpoint**

b) that the story reflects a particular culture or country's history?

6 Have you ever read anything like this before? Is it the kind of writing you would normally read?

7 Did this extract make you want to read on? Why? Why not?

Vocabulary

flats: flat fields

woodarchies/marbus: mythical evil spirits in Aboriginal culture

Key term

viewpoint: the attitude or feelings a writer or character has towards people or events

Exploring narrative perspective

You will learn how to:
• discuss and compare the different ways in which writers approach narratives with similar themes.

Narratives are often told from different perspectives, even when they deal with similar themes.

Explore

Read these three short extracts. All three texts present one character's view of the world. But what **narrative perspective** is used in each story?

Key term

narrative perspective: the viewpoint from which a story is told

Text A

> For the three runaways, the fence was a symbol of love, home and security.
>
> 'We're nearly home,' said Molly without realising they had merely reached the halfway mark, they had almost eight hundred kilometres still to go.
>
> 'We found the fence now. It gunna be easy,' she told her younger sisters.
>
> From *Follow the Rabbit-Proof Fence* by Doris Pilkington/Nugi Garimara

Text B

> 'Matilda. Matilda. Come back im-me-diately! What on earth have you got on your head? It looks like a tea cosy. And why have you got that mane of hair on your forehead.'
>
> 'I can't come back. Mother. I'll be late for my lesson.'
>
> 'Come back immediately!'
>
> She won't. She won't. She hates Mother.
>
> From 'The Wind Blows' by Katherine Mansfield

Text C

> Friday
>
> I went to school today, so I could pick up my exam results. I did really well, better than everyone expected, especially Dad. But it's bad news because he wants me to follow my dream: to be a professional footballer. More like *his* dream. He never made it 'cos of injuries. I mean, I feel for him but it's my life, isn't it? I know Mum gets it, but Dad – he reckons I'm the next Big Thing. Well, I'm not, but what can I tell him? I just don't know.
>
> From 'A Life in Danny's Day' by Mike Gould

1 Copy and complete this table, ticking the correct rows for each text.

Features	Text A	Text B	Text C
told from first-person perspective (i/we)			
told from third-person perspective (he/she/they/dan)			
reveals inner thoughts/feelings			
uses speech and dialogue to explore feelings			

2 Which of the three extracts gives you the most complete view of a character's feelings and **motives**? Why?

Key term

motive: the reason for behaving in a particular way

Develop

While not all stories told from a child's viewpoint feature conflict with adults, it is a fairly common theme. In *Follow the Rabbit-Proof Fence*, the children have escaped from a place to which they had been forced to go by adults in authority.

3 In pairs, discuss the reasons for conflict in extracts B and C. Find any words, phrases or sentences that reveal what the source of the conflict is.

4 Write a sentence about each extract explaining what the conflict is. Use these sentence starters.

> In Text B, the narrator and her mother argue about….

> In Text C, the disagreement is between the writer and…

Key term

connective: a linking word or phrase used in a sentence (e.g. 'and', 'but', 'or', 'so', 'then', 'because', 'after')

When you write about two texts, you can use **connectives** to compare or contrast. For example:

> In the first extract, Molly tells her sisters 'It's gunna be easy' — The quotation used to back this point up.
> to get home. She seems very hopeful. However, Danny is less — The point made about Molly's feelings.
> positive about his situation, saying passing his exams is — The connective that introduces how Danny is different.
> 'bad news'. — The quotation used to back this contrasting point up.

Respond

5 Write two sentences comparing Matilda's and Danny's feelings about their mothers. Include one quotation for each person.

Start: Matilda clearly feels…

Exploring how writers create children's voices and viewpoints

You will learn how to:
- explain how writers use a range of different techniques to reveal voice and viewpoint
- make efficient notes about some of these techniques.

When we read great stories, it feels like we can actually hear the character's **voice** and see things from their viewpoint. But how do writers achieve this?

Key term

voice: the distinctive way a story is told from a character's perspective

Explore

When you comment on voice, you write about the tone or manner in which a character recounts events or speaks to others. For example, look at these adjectives:

> tense anxious chatty thoughtful commanding
> positive negative humorous lively sad
> hopeful hopeless spiteful dramatic gloomy
> light-hearted angry strong mysterious
> weak passionate bitter powerful

Looking closely at the words and phrases used by a specific character or the **narrator** will help you to identify and comment on their voice and tone.

Key term

narrator: the person telling the story or recounting what happened

For example, look at how one student has annotated this short extract from Unit 4.3.

'Come back immediately !'	gives order
	'immediately' – 'this moment'
She won't. She won't. She hates Mother.	'!' exclamation

① How would you describe the mother's 'voice' based on these annotations? Copy and complete this sentence, using one or more of the adjectives from the box:

> The mother's voice comes across as ... because of the
> way she...

Voice is very closely linked to viewpoint. Look at the words and sentences used to convey Matilda's viewpoint. Although this story appears to be told in the third person, Matilda's voice comes through very powerfully in the narration too. The strong verb 'hates' tells us her viewpoint very directly.

And the repeated refusal 'She won't.' suggests a stubborn or angry tone.

Here is another extract from the same story.

> The wind, the wind. It's frightening to be here in her room by herself. The bed, the mirror, the white jug and basin gleam like the sky outside. It's the bed that is frightening. There it lies, sound asleep... Does Mother imagine for one moment that she is going to darn all those stockings knotted up on the quilt like a coil of snakes? She's not. No, Mother. I do not see why I should...
>
> From 'The Wind Blows' by Katherine Mansfield

2 Using a copy of the extract, highlight or list any words or phrases that suggest:

   a) a weak or uncertain voice

   b) a strong, defiant voice.

3 Now consider 'viewpoint'.

   a) What does her mother want Matilda to do?

   b) What is Matilda's view about this?

4 What simile indicates that she sees the stockings in a very negative way? Why is it effective?

Develop

Voice can be conveyed by both the vocabulary and the type of sentences the writer uses.

For example, look at these examples from 'A Life in Danny's Day'.

Key terms

informal language: a more personal, chatty way of writing or speaking

slang: informal language, often common to a particular group of people (e.g. teens)

Vocabulary or sentence type	Effect	Example
informal language (including abbreviations and **slang**)	sounds like the way a teenager would speak or write	''cos', 'reckons'
questions	suggest uncertainty	'...what can I tell him?'
short simple sentences	can be used for a change of tone or to sum up feelings	'I just don't know.'
compound sentences	can be used to link or explain two actions or feelings	'I went to school today, so I could pick up my exam results.'
complex sentences	can be used to explore or develop a view or feeling	'I'm going to tell Dad tonight that I'm giving up football, even though he'll be mad with me.'

Now reread this extract from Danny's diary.

> He never made it 'cos of injuries. I mean, I feel for him but it's my life, isn't it? I know Mum gets it, but Dad – he reckons I'm the next Big Thing. Well, I'm not, but what can I tell him?

5 How would you describe Danny's voice based on these sentences? Look at the highlighted words and phrases and then look at the 'voice word bank' on page 122.

Start:

I think Danny speaks in a... way. He seems ...

6 Reading the whole 'Danny' extract, what do you think his viewpoint is?

 a) How does he feel about his exam results?

 b) What does he think about his father?

 c) How are his voice and viewpoint different from Matilda's?

Read the following extract from *Follow the Rabbit-Proof Fence*, the novel about three sisters who run away from the Settlement they have been forced to live in.

Vocabulary

boomers: adult male kangaroos

indi: isn't it

Dgudu: elder sister

fullahs: fellows

The two smaller girls felt threatened by the size of the big **boomers** so they were glad to be out of sight. **1** They didn't want to be attacked by kangaroos, and they were very relieved when they had climbed the boundary fence. It was only then that they could feel safe again. The three girls sat on a fallen log, trying to recover from the shocking sight of the fighting animals.

'Those boomers are bigger than the ones we got at home, **indi Dgudu**,' said Gracie fearfully, 'and cheeky **fullahs** too.'

Daisy and Molly both answered together. 'Youay.'

The trio sat quietly on the dead log. **2** The silence was broken suddenly by an alarmed Molly, who pulled Gracie up roughly by the arms. **3**

'Run under that big tree over there **4** ,' she yelled, pointing to a large banksia tree. 'Climb up and hide there. You too Daisy. Come on.'

From *Follow the Rabbit-Proof Fence*
by Doris Pilkington/Nugi Garimara

7 Working in pairs, decide which of the highlighted sentences is a:

    a) simple sentence

    b) compound sentence

    c) complex sentence

    d) command.

8 Now identify which of these sentences:

    a) sums up the children's mood

    b) explains why the children wanted to hide

    c) tells us how Molly speaks to her sisters

    d) describes two things Molly suddenly does.

One further important aspect of this text is its use of **accent** and **dialect**. These are often linked to the use of **non-standard English**.

9 What examples of accent or dialect can you identify in the text?

10 Discuss these questions with a partner:

    a) Which parts of the text are mostly written in standard English (rather than using non-standard forms)?

    b) How does accent or dialect add to your enjoyment of the story or understanding of the characters?

> **Respond**

11 Write a paragraph about how the writer conveys the girls' feelings through the use of viewpoint or voice.

Checklist for success

✔ Start with a comment on their perspective or viewpoint on the situation.

✔ Add a sentence on how their voice is shown (you could comment on one sister's voice or all of them).

✔ Finish with a comment on how their 'childishness' is shown.

Key terms

accent: how spoken language sounds in different places (sometimes shown by different spellings – for example, 'Gwan' for 'Go on' in Caribbean English)

dialect: grammar or vocabulary specific to a place (e.g. 'cobber' is a word meaning 'friend' in Australia)

non-standard English: English that features local or socially different grammar or vocabulary from standard English

Investigating character with hot-seating

You will learn how to:

- explore a character's feelings through questioning and imagination
- adapt what you say to convey a character's experience convincingly.

Hot-seating is when you imagine you are a character from a story and answer questions that others ask you. This activity can help to develop your understanding of a character's feelings and viewpoint.

Explore

Look back to Unit 4.1 and Unit 4.3 and remind yourself about the character of Molly, the eldest of the three girls who run away from the Settlement and walk 1600 kilometres back to their homeland.

 1 Read the following extract in groups of four, with a group member taking on each 'speaking role' as Molly, Daisy or Gracie. The other group member should read the description.

One day about midday, when the sun was high in the azure sky, Daisy and Gracie heard an excited shriek from Molly who, as usual, was walking ahead of them.

'Here it is. I've found it. Come and look,' she yelled as she laughed and waved her arms.

'What is it?' asked Gracie, 'What are you shouting for?'

'I've found the rabbit-proof fence. See,' she said, pointing to the fence. 'This will take us all the way home to Jigalong.'

'But how do you know that's the rabbit-proof fence, Dgudu?' asked Daisy, with a puzzled look on her face. She didn't notice anything special about this fence.

'This fence is straight, see,' Molly explained. 'And it's clear on each side of the fence.'

She should know, after all her father was the inspector of the fence and he told her all about it. Now the fence would help her and her sisters find their way home. There was much excitement when the girls at last reached the rabbit-proof fence.

From when she was young, Molly had learned that the fence was an important landmark for the Mardudjara people of the Western Desert who migrated south from the remote regions.

From Follow the Rabbit-Proof Fence by Doris Pilkington/Nugi Garimara

---

2 How does a group reading like this help you to understand the text?

   a) How does having a different student reading each character's words help you to understand their voice, thoughts and feelings?

   b) In what way, as a performer, can you use clues in the text to convey your character?

3 What have you learned about Molly from your reading? For example, how does Molly feel when she sees the fence? What words and phrases tell you this?

Before you begin a hot-seating task, it is important to know the character and the text you are exploring well.

4 Write answers to the following questions.

   a) Who 'gives an excited shriek'? What does this tell us about the character's feelings?

   b) In the same paragraph, how does the same character show her excitement through her actions?

   c) What has she found?

   d) How does she know what it is?

   e) Why is finding this so important?

5 What evidence is there that Molly is the leader of the girls? Copy and complete the table below.

where she walks – compared with the others	
how she responds to questions	
how the others react to molly knowing about the fence	

When role-playing a character, it is useful to think about their feelings at different stages of the story.

6   Consider what Molly's thoughts and feelings might be at different points. Record your thoughts in a grid like this:

Point in the story	Thoughts and feelings
at the settlement	
in the middle of the journey of 1600 kilometres	
finding the fence	

7   Work in small groups. Choose one person to play the part of Molly in the hot-seat. The rest of you should write down the questions you want to ask her. Aim to explore how Molly might feel about having to lead her sisters. For example:

> How did you feel at the start of the journey after you'd left the Settlement?

> Why did you feel so happy when you saw the fence?

8   When everyone has decided on their questions, put them to Molly. If you are playing Molly:

a) imagine how you would feel if you had to lead two younger sisters across a wilderness

b) decide how you would speak and act or use gestures. Would you do so confidently or timidly and hesitantly? Would you sit up straight or slouch? How would you communicate your emotions to people who have not been through your experience?

9 Once you have finished, evaluate how well your group member carried out the role of Molly.

a) Did they respond in a way that matched what you know about Molly?

b) How did their actions or way of speaking convey Molly's feelings?

Exploring alternative forms and structures for stories

You will learn how to:
- identify different story forms and structures
- comment on the effect of using alternative ways of structuring stories.

You have already seen how stories can be told from different viewpoints and with different voices. But stories can also use alternative forms and structures to interest the reader.

Explore

Look at these alternative forms for the same story.

Text A

> To: jared.davis@geemail.com
>
> Dear Uncle,
>
> So, how is life on the other side of the world? I know it's your winter now, but it's the end of the exam season here – and, guess what? I got my results. I wish you'd been here when I opened them. You helped me so much, especially when I was getting into trouble…

Text B

> **Danny**
> So, I went down to the school that morning and collected my results. It was a weird day; end of August but there was this bitter wind, and the envelope was blown out of my hands and I found myself running along the road trying to catch it. By the time I captured it, I was outside the school gates, and I saw this girl on the other side of the street. I say 'girl' – I had no idea how old she was. She looked like she was homeless.
>
> **Suki**
> I'd been chucked out of the house for a month. I'd made myself a sort of little tent by the side of the road near that school. Not my old one, of course. But a good place. The rich parents picking up their kids often gave me a bit of change. But that day was exam results day. And there was this boy – it made me laugh – chasing an envelope down the road…

Text C

> Monday 15th June
>
> First day of my exams. Surprised myself by actually being organised. Pen: check! Spare pen: check! Revision notes: check! Even managed to get the earlier bus so I was at school in good time. Pat on the back, Danny. Course, all this helped when I opened the paper and saw the questions. Tough or what? But – I think I nailed it. Yep, me – Danny the joker. Me, the one everyone says only likes sport. I *nailed* it! I'm so, so pleased, man. 9 o'clock now. Mum's out but I'll tell her when she gets in.

1 Decide which one of the texts is:

   a) a diary entry

   b) a novel with **dual narrators**

   c) a story told in emails.

Key term

dual narrators: two narrators who take turns to tell the story from their viewpoint

2 As a reader, each of these approaches creates different effects. Decide which story:

   a) feels like it is addressed to the reader personally

   b) gives the impression of happening now – or just now

   c) provides alternative viewpoints on the same events.

The form the writer chooses can affect how you read the story. In the examples above, email is used as one approach. In the past, this might have been in the form of a traditional letter.

Look at the different forms and perspectives you can choose from as a writer.

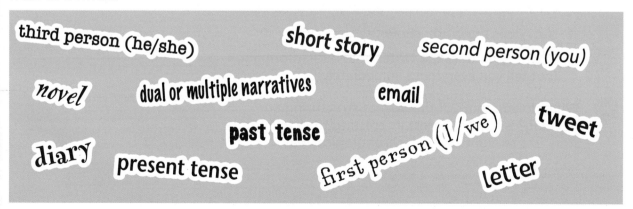

3 Think of a well-known story or film plot. Choose an alternative way to tell it using one of the forms and narrative voices above.

The structure of a text is the overall organisation of the plot and how the events are revealed. For example:

- *the time order*: Is the story **chronological**? Or does it jump from the present back to past events? Or flash-forward to future events?

- *the setting*: Does the story stay in one location or switch between different places?

- *the narrative perspective*: This is linked to the form, but a story might have just one narrator or move between different narrators.

- *the plot*: Does the writer tell the reader everything, or hold back information for effect? Does the story follow the usual sequence of introduction, development, climax, falling action, resolution?

Read this alternative opening to 'A Life in Danny's Day'.

Key term

chronological: written and organised in the order in which events happened

---

June 15th, 2050

He speaks into the mic-pad which is inserted in his wrist. 'Tell me what was happening thirty years ago today,' he commands it. A voice he knows begins to speak. The voice of a 16-year-old boy. 'First day of my exams. Surprised myself by being organised...'

He straps himself into the cube chair, which floats in the airless pod, and listens. He is taken back to that time so long ago, a time when you could still get paper. The young voice continues: '...being organised. Pen: check! Spare pen: check! Revision notes: check!'

---

4 a) Where is the main character as this story begins?

b) When does it begin? How does the time change?

c) How does the writer show the time-shifts?

d) In what way does the writer hold back information (not tell you everything immediately)?

5 What do you think of this way of structuring an opening? Is it more or less interesting than telling the story in a straightforward, chronological way?

You have already been introduced to the idea of dual narratives, when two narrators tell their version of the same story. Now read this entry from another narrator of 'A Life in Danny's Day'. It should be read alongside Text C above.

Monday 15th July

So, Daniel had his first exam today. He seemed to be very organised, which was surprising, but I suppose that's good. He seems to be spending every spare hour revising, and he says he did very well in the exam today as a result. I know this is what school wants him to do, but I'm worried because he has missed football training. He has a trial with Glenthorn United on Friday – my old club – and I'm concerned he will not be ready. If he really wants to make it as a professional footballer, he can't afford to miss opportunities like this. I had my chance once, but that knee injury scuppered everything. I'll have a word with Judith when she gets in, but she's on his side.

How does using a different narrator add something to the story? First, explore how it works: the diary starts off by mentioning the same things as Danny's diary entry – how Danny was organised for his exam. However, after that it changes.

6 a) What does 'I suppose that's good' suggest about how this writer feels about Danny being 'very organised'?

   b) Why is the writer 'worried' he is spending so much time revising?

   c) What event hasn't yet happened?

   d) Who is on Danny's side, according to the writer?

   e) Who is writing this diary entry? How do you know?

7 Why do you think the writer used different narrators? What does it add to the story? Write a paragraph explaining your thoughts. Think about:

   • how using multiple narrators adds to the drama – showing the possible conflicts in the family

   • how it might make a reader feel more or less sympathetic to a character.

Respond

8 Write a further diary extract. Imagine Danny's mother (Judith) writes a diary entry after she comes home at 9 p.m. You can choose to make it like Danny's father's entry – fairly formal and full of longer sentences. Or you could make it slightly more informal and chatty (though perhaps not as chatty as Danny's!).

Developing a character's voice and viewpoint

You will learn how to:
- write in a way that makes your character believable and stand out
- create your own convincing voice for a story.

It is important when you create characters that their voice – their way of speaking or telling the story – is consistent and individual.

Explore

Read this extract from the real-life diary of a girl who has travelled to France in 1821. In this extract, she attends a French school.

> The girls stained all their frocks and aprons with ink; if the rulers were inky they wiped them on their aprons, and if there were not **inkstands** enough, they had a very short **expedient**; they made an inkstand of the table, by pouring some ink on it into which they dipped their pens. The paper of the room was torn off, so that in many places one could see the canvas that covered the walls. Round the room were hung several maps, which looked as if they had been nibbled away by mice. The girls jumped over the stools, spirted ink at one another, tossed about the books, and danced upon the tables; it did not seem to be in the teachers' power to make them be quiet, though they sometimes gave them verses to write; but the most common punishment was either making them kneel down (which the girls seemed to think good fun), or else sending for the bonnet de nuit, which they put on and laughed.
>
> From *The Diary of a Girl in France in 1821* by Mary Browne

Vocabulary

inkstands: small trays with an inkpot and place to prop up quill pens

expedient: practical method

bonnet de nuit: night-cap (to show who the 'naughty' child is)

We often learn about a character from their observations of others.

1. In this extract, what does the writer have to say about:
   a) the behaviour of the French pupils
   b) their clothing and appearance
   c) how they react to being punished?

2 The writer also comments on the surroundings.

    a) What does she say about the maps on the walls?

    b) What does this suggest about the school?

Develop

At the start of the diary, the girl describes her family's arrival in Calais. Here are some of the phrases she uses.

cold	disagreeable	alas!	ugliest countryside	scarcely a tree to be seen
no pretty cottages	dirty	miserable	looked exactly like a desert
no hedgerows		a most charming place!	north and east winds

3 What do these impressions tell us about her views of France? For example, what can you **infer** from the phrase 'scarcely a tree to be seen'?

    a) that the French cut down all their trees

    b) that the countryside is boring

    c) that the countryside is lifeless

The language used here is formal **standard English**, and reflects how an educated child of the time might have written.

Key terms

infer: to work out what someone is implying through their choice of words

standard English: the most widely used form of English which is not specific to a particular place or region

4 Compare these two versions of a sentence from the text. Which sounds like it was written by a child today? Which sounds like a child in the nineteenth century?

    a) It did not seem to be in the teachers' power to make them be quiet.

    b) The teachers just couldn't shut the kids up.

Respond

5 Now use the words and phrases above Question 3 to build a picture of Calais and the countryside around it to write the girl's diary entry of her family's arrival in France. Use these sentence starters and try to maintain the girl's voice, using the same style of standard English.

> It is very cold…
>
> We had expected a delightful climate but…
>
> Around Calais is the…

Using punctuation to develop character

You will learn how to:
- use punctuation to add detail to your characters' voices
- use punctuation to connect ideas about characters.

In your narrative writing, you can use different types of punctuation to help you add detail and to link ideas. This can help you create more interesting and detailed characters.

Explore

1. Read these alternative ways of expressing thoughts from a character's perspective. Which thought do you prefer? Why?

   a) Gracie wondered what they would do if they were stopped by police. She often had daydreams like this. She knew Molly found it frustrating.

   b) Gracie wondered what they would do if they were stopped by police; she often had daydreams like this – Molly, she knew, found it frustrating.

The first set of thoughts uses three simple sentences. They give the reader all the information they need, but they sound rather clumsy and uninteresting. The second set uses **parenthetical punctuation** to add information and a **semicolon** to link ideas. This makes the second set more fluent.

You can add information or an opinion using parenthetical commas. For example:

> Gracie was frightened by the huge kangaroos. Martha was also scared.
>
> Martha, like her sister, was frightened by the huge kangaroos.

2. Use parenthetical commas to turn these examples into single sentences.

   a) Danny writes a diary. His dad writes a diary as well.

   Danny, …

   b) Molly made them all climb the banksia tree. She was used to getting her own way.

   Molly, who…

Key terms

parenthetical punctuation: pairs of commas, dashes or brackets that create a subordinate to add detail or personal opinion

semicolon (;): used to connect two independent clauses (clauses that could each be a sentence on their own)

Pairs of dashes and brackets create the effect of a bigger pause in the sentence than pairs of commas. For example:

> The attic door was closed – no one had used it in years – but she knew she had to go in.

This information takes us briefly away from the action to an observation about the door itself, which adds to the drama.

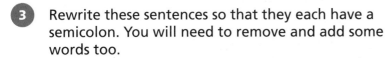

Develop

You can use semicolons to link ideas about characters and show how they are connected. For example:

> Molly had gone outside; it was raining.

This shows that Molly had gone outside *while* it was raining.

3 Rewrite these sentences so that they each have a semicolon. You will need to remove and add some words too.

a) Gracie was transfixed by the fighting kangaroos who were like giants.

b) I told mum about my exam results while we were having a cup of late-night cocoa.

c) The French children were clearly planning something as they sniggered and looked down at their disgusting desks when the teacher came in.

Respond

4 Link the following sentences in a continuous paragraph. Use parenthetical punctuation to add information and opinion. Use semicolons to link ideas.

a) Molly hated the Settlement.

b) She had two sisters.

c) They were hundreds of miles from her homeland.

d) The homeland was the place they knew and loved.

e) The rabbit-proof fence would be their guide.

f) It was straight and easy to follow.

g) Now all they had to do was find it.

Begin:

Molly, who…

Structuring your own viewpoint narrative

You will learn how to:
- develop your own story structure.

In this chapter, you have studied stories told in a range of ways, in different forms and with different narrative voices. However, it is important to remember that most stories share the same underlying pattern.

Explore

Read part of the structure for 'A Life in Danny's Day'.

Section	Details
Beginning: the scene is set, the situation/character introduced	Danny picks up his exam results; he's done well, but he's worried about his dad's reaction. His dad wants him to leave school and pursue a football career.
Rising action/complication: the main character/s begin to face obstacles or problems	Danny tells his mum, who is pleased for him. She wants him to stay on at college. But how can he tell his dad? Especially with a trial for a professional club coming up.
Climax: the most dramatic or emotional point	The day of the trial. Danny does really well. The football coach tells Danny and his dad that Danny will probably be offered an apprenticeship. But he'll need to leave school and live away from home. Danny runs off – upset. He doesn't want to leave home or pursue a football career. He shouts at his dad, telling him he only cares about his own failed career as a footballer.
Falling action: tension reduces as things begin to get worked out	Dad tracks Danny down at the local park. He is sitting on a park bench.
End: questions are answered, but not necessarily a happy ending	

1. How might the story end?
   a) Will Dad listen to Danny? Or will he force him to leave school?
   b) How might Danny's mum help?
   c) Will the story end happily or badly – or somewhere in between?

2 Now share your ideas with a partner. **Synthesise** the best ideas from both and agree on what would make the best ending. Remember:

- an effective ending does not necessarily mean a happy one
- the ending should fit logically with what has gone before – don't suddenly have Danny being abducted by aliens!

Key term
....
synthesise: bring together ideas from two different sources

Develop

As you saw in Unit 4.5, different types of structure create different effects.

3 Match each technique to the correct example below.

Flashback: this is where the story goes back in time to earlier events.	I stared at the envelope, and tore it open. I'd passed! All my exams…
	I sat on the bench and waited for Dad to speak, but he just stared at me. He didn't know what to say. … When I got to the park, Danny was sitting on the bench, staring into the distance. I approached, but the words stuck in my throat. I couldn't say 'sorry'.
In media res: this is when the story begins in the heart of the action.	
Framed narrative: this is when a story is contained within a story.	I sat on the park bench. The memories came flooding back. That time when, aged three, I'd first kicked a football with Dad. It had been a rainy day and…
	The robot park-keeper pulled the metal capsule out of the earth and wrenched off the lid. Inside was an old papery thing. The robot did not know what it was but pulled back the rotting cover.
Parallel stories: where two stories run alongside each other.	Tuesday 15th August 2020. Dad is so annoying…

Respond

4 A student needs help with his story called 'The Decision'. In the story, a talented teenage musician has been selected to go to an expensive music school in another town, but it means leaving his or her friends behind.

What structure would you choose? Choose one or more techniques and explain why it would work.

Writing a key moment from a child's viewpoint

You will learn how to:
- write a section from a story which will interest the reader
- apply all the different narrative writing skills you have learned.

Your task

You are now going to write your own section of a story told from a child's point of view. You can choose your own title, but the story must be based around a difficult decision or choice, and a young person (aged 15 or under) must be the main character or narrator.

Approaching the task

First, you will need to get some ideas for your story. You can use techniques you have learned in this chapter or in Stage 7 to generate ideas. You can also use any of the ideas that have come up in this chapter if you like.

1 Make notes or create a spider diagram. One should be for the plot aspect for 'The Decision', as shown below.

What is it to do with? Friends? Work? School? Money? — The Decision — [ ] — Made by…

2 Next, focus on your main character. You could look back at Unit 1 to help you with ideas, and think about characters you have come across in this chapter. You could use an index-style card, like the one below.

Name:

Age:

Appearance:

Character traits (what he/she is like):

3 Now create your plot plan using a grid like the one below. How you structure it will come after this.

Section	Details
Beginning	Amal has saved a lot of money through babysitting for her aunt. But now she has a big decision – buy the thing she's always wanted or…
Rising action/ complication	
Climax	
Falling action	
End	

4 Once you have your plot, think about the structure. How will you tell or reveal your story? Think about all the possible narrative structures you have explored in this chapter. For example: flashback, framed or dual narratives, beginning *in media res*.

Make brief notes on your choice, and how this would affect your story.

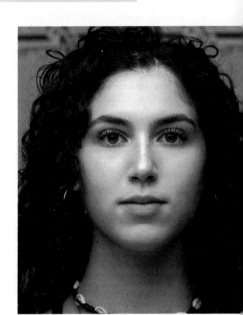

5 What form will you choose for your story? Choose from one of these options:

- a standard prose short story
- in diary or diaries form
- in email, letter or letters form
- another form – can you think of a different one?

6 Now, think about the narrative perspective and your character's or narrator's voice. Here are some of your choices:

- first-, second- or third-person narrative
- present or past tense, or switching between the two
- accent or dialect
- formal or informal language – or a mix of them.

7. Choose the section of the story you are going to focus on and write at least 100 words of it. If you are still stuck for ideas, you can use this opening. It comes from the 'rising action' part of the story.

> Amal stood outside the shop window and stared in. Wow. The camera looked amazing. Okay, her camera-phone was cool, but let's face it, not the best for proper, professional shots. The problem was the price, obviously.

Checklist for success

✔ Make sure you maintain the same voice, unless you have two narrators.

✔ Make it clear what part of the story you are telling.

✔ Choose punctuation, such as use of dashes or other creative choices, to say something about the narrator or the action, such as how dramatic it is.

✔ Use a variety of sentences for impact, for example, short and sharp for pace and drama.

✔ Use time connectives to show the chronology of what is happening.

✔ Use any strategies you know to ensure you spell key words accurately.

✔ Consider how you can vary vocabulary by altering the part of speech. For example: *Amal felt **envy**/was **envious**/**envied** her friend/**enviously** eyed.*

Reflecting on your work

8. Compare your own response to Question 7 to the two responses below. Using the comments, identify ways in which your own response could be improved and rewrite it, if needed.

Response 1

Tuesday

I know we have to move because of Dad's job, but I don't want to. I mean, it's not fair. I have all my friends. I've known loads of them from primary school. When Mum told me today I ran out of the house as I was so upset and then I went round to Ricky's but he wasn't there. So I ended up walking the streets like a zombie and then got the bus home as there wasn't much else I could do. Mum says it's not fair too as she likes her job and she's got to give it up.

Wednesday

Dad had a big chat with me this evening after supper. Dad told me I was being selfish.

Gives sense of informal voice but sentences not varied enough.

Time phrase helps the order of the story.

Effective simile but rather unoriginal.

New entry moves story on.

Comment on Response 1

The narrator's voice is well-established, but the lack of variety in sentence structure and the lack of other descriptive detail makes this a little dull to read.

Response 2

The drought had lasted six months. Abby's mother had forbidden them to take any water from the fridge, but that night, Abby couldn't stop thinking about the last bottle of water, ice cold, in the fridge door. It was so hot! She sat up in bed and stared at her sleeping sister. Just a little sip – that's all she would need.

After sitting there for ten minutes, trying to make up her mind, she swung her legs out of bed. She started to walk across the bedroom floor, but every step made a terrible creak. What if her parents caught her? Well, it was worth it.

Effective opening sentence grabs the reader's attention.

Detail establishes time setting.

Variety of sentences convey narrator's emotions.

New paragraph moves story on.

Questioning and response help create character.

Comment on Response 2

The writer efficiently fills in background detail of the story while allowing the reader to follow what is happening now. The variety of sentences and use of punctuation both add to the characterisation and the drama.

Responding to a narrative text

You will learn how to:
- write about the techniques a writer uses to convey a child's perspective
- improve your own responses in the light of sample answers.

You are going to explore the ways in which the text you read at the start of this chapter works, using the understanding you have built up in this chapter. In particular, you will look at voice and viewpoint, especially the way in which children see the world.

Understanding the text

Reread the extract from *Follow the Rabbit-Proof Fence* from Unit 4.1.

1. Write a sentence in response to each of these questions.

   a) Explain in your own words where and when the extract takes place, and how you know this.

   b) Find at least one phrase or sentence that tells you how Molly feels about the Settlement and being so far from home.

   phrase(s) or sentence: _____

   feeling: _____

   c) Copy and complete this sentence explaining in your own words what happens at the end of the extract.

   > The extract ends with Molly saying that they can't stay in the Settlement because…

Thinking about the text's purpose and features

2. Look again at the extract. Which aspects of a child-centred narrative story can you find? Copy and complete the grid with the relevant line numbers.

Feature	Line number/s
children's relationships with each other/family members	
inner thoughts or feelings	
questioning the world around them	
fearing or misunderstanding the world	
speaking in a child-like way	

3 Several characters are mentioned in the extract.

a) Who are they?

b) Whose viewpoints or attitudes do we find out about?

4 Only one of these girls has a developed sense of voice: we see inside her mind and feelings and hear her speak about events.

a) Who is it?

b) What does she comment on?

5 The writer of the book is the real-life daughter of Molly. She, like her mother, was removed to a Settlement far away from home. Why do you think she chose to write this book?

Looking at the text in detail

In the extract, there are several words and phrases that tell the reader about the girls' responses to what is happening.

6 In the first paragraph, what phrase suggests the river they are looking at is impressive and contrasts with their own homeland?

7 What does Molly mean when she says, 'We are all cut off from our families'? Consider each of these possibilities and choose one.

a) totally separated from   b) rejected by

c) injured by   d) not speaking to

8 The writer uses a range of vocabulary to create a vivid picture of the Australian setting.

a) Molly mentions three different types of water feature (like 'sea') back home. What are they?

b) What two species of tree does Molly mention the river 'swirling' around?

9 The writer also uses a range of sentence types and punctuation to convey what is happening or a character's thoughts.

a) Read the following sentence:

> The eldest girl, Edna Green, was showing the youngsters how to cross to the other side by using a long stick to measure the depth of the water.

What additional information has been given by using bracketing commas?

b) In the following longer sentence, bracketing commas have been used three times. Identify the examples and note down what additional information is included in each case.

> As they rounded the bend of the rough road, still stepping cautiously trying to miss the muddy puddles, they were surprised to see about six or seven girls, one aged around seventeen, with a group of girls eight years old or perhaps younger, all wading across the icy cold water.

c) Which of these additional sections:

- gives detail about the landscape and the girls' movements
- gives details about the ages of the girls?

Writing about the text

10 Reread the whole extract.

How does the writer create a sense of Molly's voice and viewpoint? You could comment on:

- her thoughts and feelings about the Settlement and home
- how she responds to the information about the 'woodarchies'.

You should try to write 75–100 words.

You could begin:

> *The reader is given a sense of Molly's viewpoint when…*

Checklist for success

✔ Make at least two clear points about how the writer conveys Molly's viewpoint.

✔ Refer to words or phrases from the extract and put them in quotation marks.

✔ Think about the choices the writer has made in terms of vocabulary, and, if relevant sentences and punctuation.

11 Compare your own response to Question 10 to the two responses below. Using the comments, identify ways in which your own response could be improved and rewrite it, if needed.

Response 1

The reader finds out about Molly's viewpoint when it says she feels like an outsider in her situation. It says 'a stranger in this part of the country'. This is because she has been separated from her family and nothing looks the same here.

Another point is that she shows she is frightened by where she is. She says woodarchies are like marbus and it is dangerous to stay in this place as they might kill them.

— Clear statement about Molly.

— Evidence is included, but not in a fluent way.

— A rather basic explanation.

— Introduces a new point.

Comment on Response 1

This response makes two clear points about how Molly views the situation. However, it does not really explore the language from the extract. Also, a quotation would make the second point more detailed.

Response 2

The reader gets a sense of Molly's viewpoint when she states that she was 'overcome with a deep longing for the dry, rugged, red landscape of the Pilbara'. The phrase 'deep longing' shows how strongly she misses her homeland. She also says she felt 'cut off', which is a powerful phrase suggesting the big gap separating her from home.

The details about how Molly speaks also give the reader an idea of her viewpoint. It says she 'whispered' when talking to the others about 'marbus' as if the 'woodarchies' could hear her. This shows she is still a child, really.

— Detailed explanation of Molly's perspective.

— Explains the phrase clearly.

— Develops the original point

— Fluently moves on to new aspect – her speech.

— Neat summary phrase.

Comment on Response 2

This response also makes two good points about Molly. The quotations are chosen carefully and the student explains their effect. There is a summary sentence at the end of the second paragraph.

What you have achieved

Reading

- You have identified how some texts reflect particular cultures or places.
- You have compared different types and forms of modern and older stories.
- You have commented on the methods used by writers to develop distinctive voices and viewpoints.

Writing

- You have learned how to develop a distinctive voice and viewpoint for characters in your own stories.
- You have used punctuation both to aid characterisation and help with story structure.
- You have been able to choose from a range of structures and forms to create your own story.

Speaking and listening

- You have used group reading aloud to help gain a picture of characters in a novel.
- You have learned to explore a character through the use of role-play.
- You have evaluated your own and others' speaking/role-play skills.

Next steps

Reading

Have you read any other stories with children as the main characters or that are narrated by them? What can you remember about the plot, characters and narrative viewpoint? Could you empathise with the children's lives? Why/why not?

You could read the rest of *Follow the Rabbit-Proof Fence* by Doris Pilkington/Nugi Garimara and find out if the girls ever reached their homes. There is also a film of the book.

A lot of Katherine Mansfield's stories are written from the viewpoint of children or young people. If you enjoyed the extracts from 'The Wind Blows', you could try reading 'The Doll's House'.

Writing

You could complete the story you wrote a section of in Unit 5.9 and then compare or share your finished work with your classmates. Did any of you create similar stories? Did anyone use an unusual or original structure?

Speaking and listening

How would an oral diary be different from a written one? You could record or speak aloud short spoken entries about your life or experiences on particular days. To be even more creative, create an oral diary for someone else. How would they speak? What would they say?

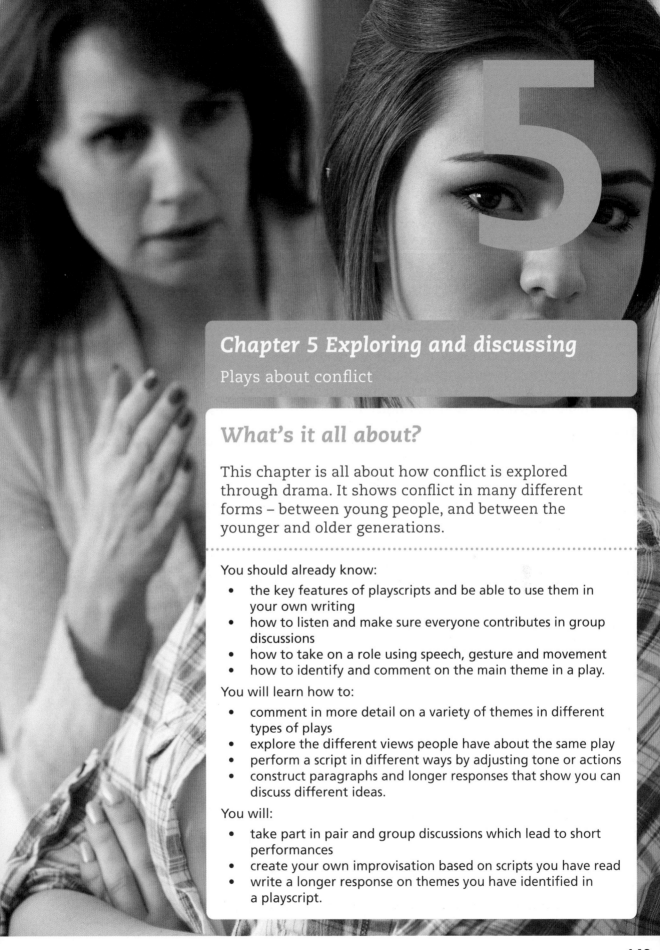

Chapter 5 Exploring and discussing

Plays about conflict

What's it all about?

This chapter is all about how conflict is explored through drama. It shows conflict in many different forms – between young people, and between the younger and older generations.

You should already know:

- the key features of playscripts and be able to use them in your own writing
- how to listen and make sure everyone contributes in group discussions
- how to take on a role using speech, gesture and movement
- how to identify and comment on the main theme in a play.

You will learn how to:

- comment in more detail on a variety of themes in different types of plays
- explore the different views people have about the same play
- perform a script in different ways by adjusting tone or actions
- construct paragraphs and longer responses that show you can discuss different ideas.

You will:

- take part in pair and group discussions which lead to short performances
- create your own improvisation based on scripts you have read
- write a longer response on themes you have identified in a playscript.

Enjoy reading

You will learn how to:
- discuss your first impressions of a scene from a play.

You are going to read an extract from *I Will Marry When I Want*, a play set in Kenya by Ngugi wa Thiong'o and Ngugi wa Mirii.

1. Think about the details above and the title of the play.

   a) Judging from the play's title, what could be the conflict in the play?

   b) The play takes place in Kenya. What do you know about Kenya and the people who live there?

2. Read the extract slowly, noting down any words or phrases you do not know. The play takes place in the home of Kiguunda, a farm labourer, and his wife and daughter, Wangeci and Gathoni.

The opening stage and set directions read:

> *Kiguunda's home. A square, mud-walled, white-ochred, one-roomed house. The white **ochre** is fading. In one corner can be seen Kiguunda and Wangeci's bed. In another can be seen a pile of rags on the floor. The floor is Gathoni's bed and the rags, her bedding. Although poorly dressed, Gathoni is very beautiful. In 5 the same room can be seen a pot on three stones. On one of the walls there hangs a framed **title-deed** for one and a half acres of land. Near the head of the bed, on the wall, there hangs a sheathed sword. On one side of the wall there hangs Kiguunda's coat, and on the opposite side, on the same wall, Wangeci's 10 coat. The coats are torn and patched. A pair of **tyre sandals** and a basin can be seen on the floor.*

Vocabulary

ochre: a mixture of clay and earth used in decoration

title-deed: a certificate proving ownership of land or buildings

tyre-sandals: type of slip-on shoe made from old car tyres

madam: wife

The story so far

When this scene opens, a short way into the play, Kiguunda has just heard that they are to receive a visit from the wealthy farm owner and his wife, Kioi and Jezebel.

WANGECI:	I wonder what Mr Kioi And Jezebel, his **madam**, Want in a poor man's home?　　　　　　　　15 Why did they take all that trouble to let us know beforehand That they would be coming here today?

KIGUUNDA: You, you woman,
            Even if you see me in these tatters
            I am not poor.   20

He shows her the title-deed by pointing at it. Then he hangs it back on the wall.

            You should know
            That a man without debts is not poor at all.
            Aren't we the ones who make them rich?
            Were it not for my blood and sweat   25
            And the blood and sweat of all the other workers,
            Where would the likes of Kioi and his wife now be?
            Tell me!
            Where would they be today?
WANGECI: Leave me alone,
            You'll keep on singing the same song   30
            Till the day you people wake up.

From *I Will Marry When I Want*
by Ngugi wa Thiong'o and Ngugi wa Mirii

3 Now choose five of the words or phrases you noted down. Can you work out what each one means?

a) What sort of word is it: a verb, adjective, adverb, noun or **noun phrase**?

b) Does it contain a prefix or suffix you know already? (For example, 'im' is a prefix meaning 'not'.)

c) Does the context help? Look at the rest of the sentence – what is happening?

Key term

noun phrase: a noun with additional information, for example, with an adjective: '*hot* weather'; the noun is called the head word in a noun phrase

4 Note down answers to the following big five questions.

a) **Who** is this extract about?

b) **What** is happening in the extract?

c) **When** are the events happening: now, in the past or in the future? Can you tell?

d) **Where** do the events take place?

e) **Why** has the writer included the information about the **set** and stage design?

5 What tells you that this scene is happening in a particular place and culture?

Key term

set: the objects and designs that create the idea of a place on a stage

6 Have you ever read anything like this before? Is it the kind of writing you would normally read?

7 Did this extract make you want to see or read the rest of the play? Why? Why not?

Identifying key themes in a play

You will learn how to:
- identify the key issues or themes within a drama text
- explore different readers' responses to the same text.

Before thinking about what a play is about, or what its themes may be, you need to be clear about its plot and what is actually happening.

Explore

Read this next extract from the play you looked at in Unit 5.1.

WANGECI:	Gathoni!
GATHONI:	Yeees!
WANGECI:	Can't you help me In peeling potatoes, And sorting out the rice, Or in looking after the fire? Instead of sitting there, Legs stretched, Plaiting your hair?
GATHONI:	Mother, you love complaining Haven't I just swept the floor?
WANGECI:	And what is that bedding doing over there? Can't you put it somewhere in a corner, Or else take it outside to the sun So the fleas can fly away?
GATHONI:	These **tatters**! Are these what you call bedding? And this floor, Is this what you call a bed?
WANGECI:	Why don't you get yourself a husband Who'll buy you spring beds?
GATHONI:	Mother, why are you insulting me? Is that why you refused to send me to school, So that I may remain your slave, And for ever **toil** for you? Picking tea and coffee only for you to pocket the wages? And all that so you can get money To pay fees for your son! Do you want me to remain buried under these ashes?

From *I Will Marry When I Want* by Ngugi wa Thiong'o and Ngugi wa Mirii

Vocabulary

tatters: rags

toil: work hard doing something tiring or unpleasant

1. There are three issues which Gathoni and her mother disagree over.

   a) In what way is Gathoni not doing what her mother would like at the start of the scene?

   b) Why does Gathoni complain about her bed?

   c) How is Gathoni treated differently from her brother (according to her)?

2. Which of these themes or issues do you think the writers are exploring? Which do you think was most important to them? Find evidence for each.

   a) laziness and hard work

   b) family conflict

   c) children's ambitions and hopes

   d) education of boys and girls.

3. What other themes do you think the play addresses?

Develop

4. Later in the play, Gathoni's father says that he would not have dared to speak to his parents in the way his daughter does. In small groups, discuss the following.

   a) How would you feel as Gathoni's parent?

   b) How would you feel if you were Gathoni?

5. Make sure everyone in your group gets a chance to express their views. Then, evaluate what you have heard:

   • Did everyone agree – or were there different interpretations?

   • What were the points of agreement or disagreement?

   • In what ways have your views changed or developed now you have listened to what others say (if at all)?

Respond

6. Write a paragraph of personal response to the scene. Explain who you feel sympathy for and why.

Checklist for success

✔ This is your interpretation so it does not matter if you think differently from others.

✔ Support your point with at least one quotation from the text.

Exploring themes through contrasting characters

You will learn how to:

- explore key details to understand characterisation and themes in a play
- listen carefully and express your views in a discussion.

You can use many of the same skills when exploring plays as you do when exploring fiction or non-fiction prose texts. However, the techniques dramatists use can also provide clues about key themes, ideas or characters' relationships.

Explore

Writers use a number of different techniques to tell us about characters or relationships. Read this short extract from a play called **Running Dream** set in Dominica, an island in the Caribbean. Two sisters are arguing.

Vocabulary

nah: a dialect word meaning 'please'

Clementine:	Give me yours **nah**?
Grace:	(*Hugging her doll close*) You mad! Mine don't break – yours break, why I have to give you mine?
Clementine:	(*Thinks*) Come. (*Grace approaches Clementine cautiously holding onto her doll.*)
Grace:	What?
Clementine:	I don't want your doll nah I jus' want to see if it have a face like mine. (*Grace takes a peek at her doll's face, keeping it well out of Clementine's reach.*)

From *Running Dream* by Trish Cooke

1 What does the writer tell us directly about the plot and the characters on stage? Make brief notes under these headings.

Writer's techniques	Example	Effect or meaning
Grace's actions	(*Hugging her doll close*)	an instruction within a playscript describing how the text should be performed
Grace's speech: what does she say?		
Clementine's speech and actions		

2 What does the writer imply about the relationship between Grace and Clementine? Make your own judgement or interpretation based on what is said (the spoken lines) and the actions (**stage directions**).

Key term

stage direction: information provided by the writer of a play which tells the actor what to do or how to speak

For example: what does 'Grace approaches Clementine cautiously' suggest about how Grace feels? Is she cautious because she's worried about losing her doll? Or does she suspect Clementine in some way?

Playwrights develop **characterisation** through:

- stage directions and actions in the present tense: Grace's nervous behaviour ('approaches cautiously'); Clementine's scheming ('Thinks')

- the length and style of the spoken lines: Grace's short demands ('Give me yours nah?', 'Come')

- vocabulary choices: 'You mad!' (about Clementine).

Now read the rest of the extract.

Grace:	Yes it have a face. (*She looks at Clementine's doll*) Yes is the same thing.
Clementine:	So how you know that one is yours and this one with the mash up foot is mine?
Grace:	Because your name was mark on that parcel. You think you smart Clementine but you don't getting mine doh!
Clementine:	Gimme it! (*Clementine tries to snatch the doll. Grace runs. Clementine sits down running her fingers in the dirt. Grace notices. She comes back and sits beside her.*)
Clementine:	Is O.K. Mine is prettier anyway... (*Clementine sees a cigarette box on the floor she picks it up. There is nothing inside but the silver paper.*)
Clementine:	You have money?
(*Grace searches her pockets. She finds a coin.*)	
Grace:	Only that.
Clementine:	Let's go buy penny bread.
Grace:	One penny bread! That's all the money can buy.
Clementine:	You want to see magic. (*Clementine covers the coin with the silver paper*) We can get two bread and still get change. Come let's go by Ma Belle. (*One of the **Chorus** steps out and becomes Ma Belle. She is an old lady who cannot see too well.*)
Clementine:	(*Pushing Grace ahead of her*) You go first!
Grace:	Why me? Is always me?
Clementine:	You is the youngest.
Grace:	I always the youngest.
Clementine:	(*Pushing her in*) Jus' go on!

From *Running Dream* by Trish Cooke

3 Both extracts effectively create a picture of the relationship between Grace and Clementine. What actions does the writer include?

4 What two subjects do the sisters talk about talk about?

5 Which of the following ideas does the writer imply about the relationship between the two sisters?

a) Grace does not like Clementine.

b) Grace is bossed around by Clementine.

c) Grace mistrusts Clementine.

d) Grace is jealous of Clementine.

Read this response by a student to the question: 'How does the writer explore the relationship between Grace and Clementine in this extract?'

> The scene opens with Clementine demanding to look at Grace's doll. This suggests Clementine is the bossier of the two sisters. But Grace is not stupid, and makes sure her sister doesn't get her way on this occasion.

6 Which of the following sentences could be added to the response to provide evidence of Grace's suspicions about her sister's motives?

a) Grace tells her 'you think you smart Clementine, but you don't getting mine'.

b) Grace 'comes back and sits beside her'.

c) Grace 'searches her pocket and finds a coin'.

7 The use of **non-standard English** and dialect is also very noticeable in this extract.

a) Find at least three examples of speech using non-standard forms.

b) Note down any that are particularly revealing about Grace's or Clementine's characters and their relationship.

Key term

non-standard English: English that features local or socially different grammar or vocabulary from standard English

Develop

You are going to have a discussion about the things that are important in a friendship or sibling relationship. Think about how you could share your ideas with others and get the most out of a discussion on such a personal issue.

Make sure you show you understand others' viewpoints during the discussion. Do this by summing up what they say. For example:

> So, what you're saying is...

> Let me get this right, you believe that...

Make your opinion count, but in a positive way.

> I understand your point, but what if...?

> Have you considered this...?

8 Look at the qualities in the word bank. Which of these would you say fit Grace or Clementine? Are there any that don't fit?

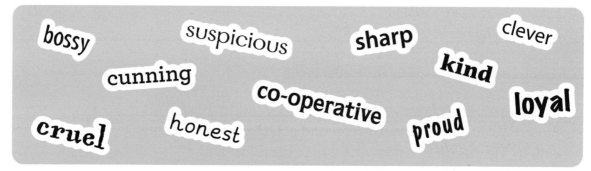

bossy   suspicious   sharp   clever

cunning   kind

co-operative   loyal

cruel   honest   proud

9 Now, get together in small groups and share your views on friendship or sibling relationships. Ask each other thoughtful questions. For example, 'What's the best thing a friend has done for you?, 'Can a rival be a friend?' or 'Who would you trust to keep a secret?'

Respond

10 Create a poster to sum up some of your ideas about the themes that you have covered in this unit.

a) In the middle, draw a picture of Grace and Clementine, based on how you imagine them from the play. Write character adjectives around each of them. Add quotations that support your adjectives.

b) At the bottom, write a paragraph about the themes explored in the extract. You could start: 'One key theme explored in the extract is ...'.

Developing your drama and discussion skills

You will learn how to:
- explore possibilities in a script through performance
- adapt ideas after discussion.

It is important that you work cooperatively with others when discussing ideas, and also help yourself and others to improve through thoughtful feedback.

Explore

Read this short scene in pairs.

> *A small stall selling fresh and dried fruit. Riad is standing behind the counter, yawning.*
>
> Father: Why are you yawning, Riad?
>
> Riad: (*grumpily*) Because I'm not supposed to be here. It was meant to be Aziz's turn.
>
> Father: Aziz is not cut out to help me set up the stall like you. He is more... academic.
>
> Riad: Academic? You mean lazy and good for nothing!
>
> Father: He was up late revising for his exams last night. I gave him the morning off.
>
> Riad: What? He wasn't revising, Dad. He was playing video games.
>
> Father: I went into his room and he was revising.
>
> Riad: Don't you realise he listens out for the creaking stairs? He hears you coming!
>
> Father: Nonsense. Aziz is a good boy at heart. I have high hopes for him. As the saying goes, 'a tree begins with a seed'.
>
> Riad: What happens if the seed is fed too much and given too much water?
>
> Father: What do you mean?
>
> Riad: You spoil him.
>
> Father: Nonsense! What is learned in youth is carved in stone.
>
> Riad: Well, he's not learning much on those video games. Anyway, what about me?
>
> Father: One day I might let you run this stall all on your own. Now – stop yawning. We have work to do.
>
> By Mike Gould

1. Work with a partner to discuss these questions. Make sure you give each other time to explain fully and do not jump in with your own point until the other has spoken.

   a) Who are the two characters in this scene?

   b) What is the conflict about?

   c) How does it end?

2. Now, consider what you need to know about each character to help you perform the script. Copy and complete the following table.

Which character...?	Riad or Father	What does this tell us?
speaks 'grumpily'		
uses sayings/proverbs to explain Aziz's behaviour		
is easily tricked by Aziz		
isn't fooled by Aziz		

3. a) What do you think the following two sayings mean? Discuss them with a partner.

   • 'a tree begins with a seed'

   • 'What is learned in youth is carved in stone.'

   b) What does Riad's father mean when he says these things about Aziz?

Now, think about how you could perform this with someone else.

4   Working on your own to begin with, on a copy of the script:

　a) highlight any words or phrases you would stress

　b) put a slanted line (/) where you would add a pause (in addition to the one shown by the ellipsis)

　c) make notes around the script suggesting any gestures or movements – for example, how might Riad show his annoyance?

5   Now, with your partner:

　a) share the script notes you have made

　b) discuss the possible ways you could perform the script

　c) between you, agree an approach in which you synthesise ideas from both your scripts.

6   Rehearse a short performance of the script and show it to another pair.

　a) What similarities and differences were there between the two performances?

　b) Was there anything you thought went particularly well in your own, and in the other pair's performances?

Develop

7   Playscripts are often open to interpretation. Try performing the playscript again in a way you haven't before, adapting your voice and actions to fit these alternatives.

　a) Riad speaks in a humorous way – he is not that upset; Father speaks in a friendly way.

　b) Riad is very angry; Father is apologetic, timid.

　c) Riad is timid; Father is bullying and aggressive.

Think about how the voices would have to change. For example, a timid Father might say: 'I... I... *umm*... gave him the morning off.'

A rude, aggressive Father might say: '*I* gave him the morning off.' (Stress the 'I' to show who is in charge.)

8 Now, in a small group, discuss the different versions of the playscript you have seen performed, and your own.

a) Which version or versions were most effective in your opinion?

b) Which were most effective in the group's opinion?

c) Why did these work so well?

Structuring a response to themes in drama

You will learn how to:
- structure a paragraph about an aspect of a play
- structure the whole of a response so it links together.

When you write about plays you have seen or read, you may need to explore more than one aspect. For example, each paragraph you write should deal with a new point or idea.

> **Explore**

You read the first part of the scene between Riad and his father in Unit 5.4. Here is the rest of scene. Read it carefully, thinking about how the key theme of conflict is developed.

Father: One day I might let you run this stall all on your own. Now – stop yawning. We have work to do.

Riad comes out from behind the counter.

Riad: Sorry, Dad: I've had enough. This is the third time this week that Aziz should've been here. And you let him off. All our lives you have spoiled my younger brother. Aziz wants a new bike? Fine – he can have one. Me? I get the old secondhand one from your uncle.

Father: That was a good bike, your uncle's.

Riad: Good? For one thing I was too little to ride it. Secondly, it was a death-trap! The brakes didn't work.

Father: You must admit it was funny when you fell off into that muddy pond. Aziz thought it was hilarious!

Riad takes off his overalls and throws them onto the stand. He begins to walk away from the stand.

Father: Riad! Where are you going? The dates and figs need putting out, and the counter needs rearranging. The market is opening soon and the customers won't be pleased if they can't get their favourite things. You can't leave me to do it all on my own!

Riad: Can't I? I'm going home to dig up your precious seed and tell him he's wanted at the stall. He can get here quickly on that bike he never uses.

Father: What about you? What are you going to do?

Riad: I'm going back to bed.

By Mike Gould

In order to write about the themes, you need to be clear about how the action and relationships develop.

 1
  a) Why is Riad particularly upset with Aziz this week?

  b) What specific example does he give about how his father has spoilt Aziz in the past?

  c) How can you tell that Riad does not find the memory of falling off the bike 'funny'?

It is also important to be able to quote specific examples to comment on the effect of language, for example, in discussing the conflict between father and son.

2 Which of these quotations, from both sections of the playscript, could be used to show that Riad resents how his father treats Aziz?

> 'I'm going back to bed', 'lazy and good for nothing', 'You spoil him', 'I've had enough', 'your precious seed', 'I get the old second-hand one', 'Aziz is a good boy', 'The dates and figs need putting out'

You could then construct a clear paragraph using the quotation. For example:

> Riad clearly has a poor opinion of his brother. When his father tries to excuse him, Riad says Aziz is 'lazy and good for nothing'. Riad is probably right to call him 'lazy' as he stays up late pretending to revise.

3 Identify the following in the paragraph above:

  a) the key point

  b) the quotation/evidence

  c) the further point or explanation.

4 Now complete this paragraph by using one of the quotations above and explaining what it tells us.

> Riad resents the fact that he has been treated differently from his brother. While Aziz was given…

You will need to make more than one point when writing about a theme in a play. It is useful to be able to structure your response so that you deal with one point after another.

5 Here is a plan for a short essay on the theme of conflict in the playscript. Copy and complete it, adding any further points of conflict, evidence to back them up, and any explanations needed.

Paragraph	Evidence/quotation	Explanation
1 Main conflict: between father and son		Father thinks Aziz is dutiful but Riad…
2 Other conflict: between brothers		Aziz is thoughtless because…
3 Any other potential conflict?		

6 Write at least one paragraph from this essay response. This will be your first draft, so you will have a chance to check it and rewrite if needed.

Before you begin, consider the vocabulary you might use in your writing. Can you spell these words correctly? What methods might you use to make sure you don't get them wrong?

theme   character   issue   conflict

playwright   playscript   staging

gesture   action   dialogue

7 Now, write your draft. You could use these sentence starters for your paragraphs:

> • The main conflict in the play is between Riad and his father. This is shown when…
>
> • Another important point of conflict is the one between the brothers. This isn't shown directly but…
>
> • Finally, the writer also hints at conflict between the father and…

Checklist for success

✔ Choose a suitable quotation that supports your point: this could be something someone says, or it could be a stage direction.

✔ Make sure you put quotation marks around the quotation you select (whether it is speech or not).

✔ Add a comment on what you learn from the language or the effect it creates, such as tension.

8 Proofread your draft.

   a) Did you spell the key words correctly?

   b) Did you use quotation marks around quotations?

   c) Did you write sentences with clear punctuation? Did you avoid the **comma splice**?

9 Write your final, redrafted paragraph.

Key term

comma splice: an error in which a sentence is divided by a comma, when a new sentence, a conjunction or a semicolon is needed (e.g. 'He got angry, the phone didn't work.')

Responding to a playscript about conflict

You will learn how to:

- explore a playwright's use of a range of techniques
- respond to how key themes in a play are presented.

You are going to explore the ways in which the text you read at the start of this chapter works, using the understanding you have built up throughout this chapter.

Make sure you reread the scene in Unit 5.1 from *I Will Marry When I Want*, carefully.

Understanding the text

1 Write a sentence in response to each of these questions.

a) Explain in your own words where and when the scene takes place, and how you know this.

b) Find at least one phrase that tells you how Kiguunda feels about their situation.

Phrase(s): ....

Feeling: ....

c) Find at least one phrase that tells you how Wangeci feels about Kiguunda.

Phrase(s): ....

Feeling: ....

d) Copy and complete this sentence, explaining in your own words what is about to happen in the next stage of the play.

> In the scene, Kiguunda and his wife are ...

Thinking about the text's purpose and features

2 The form of the text is a playscript, but it is divided into two main sections.

a) What is the purpose of the section of text from the start up to '...a basin can be seen on the floor.'? Write a sentence in response.

b) How is the second part of the extract different (from 'I wonder what Mr Kioi...' onwards)?

3 Which of the following features tell you that this is:

a) a playscript

b) set in a particular culture or place?

Add line numbers to show where you noted this. One example in each case will do. Take care: not all of these are features of playscripts!

Feature	Line numbers/quotation
gives details of the set or staging	
gives details of props, costumes, appearance, etc.	
uses speech marks	
has characters' actions in the present tense	
is divided into chapters	
uses some non-standard english grammar	
uses names that suggest a particular country or place	

Looking at the text in detail

4 Many of the details of the hut and the characters' appearance suggest they are poor.

a) What phrase describing the coats in the opening stage directions suggests that they have been worn and repaired many times?

b) Which word does Kiguunda use in lines 18–20 that tells us his clothes are falling apart?

5 One of the themes of the play is conflict.

a) In what way does Kiguunda disagree with his wife when she says they live in a 'poor man's home'? Copy and complete this sentence:

> Kiguunda disagrees by stating…

b) There are a number of potential conflicts in the play, which you can see in this scene. Which of the following do you think are evident here? Make sure you base your answer only on what you have read in this scene.

Kiguunda and his wife disagree about being poor. ☐

Kioi and Jezebel don't like Kiguunda and Wangeci. ☐

Poor people resent how the rich got rich because of their hard work.

☐

Wangeci is fed up of Kiguunda always complaining.

☐

Gathoni is ashamed of her parents being so poor.

☐

c) Kiguunda uses a number of **rhetorical questions** to get his point across. What does he mean by this speech:

> KIGUUNDA: Where would the likes of Kioi and his wife now be?
> Tell me!
> Where would they be today?

Answer in your own words.

Writing about the text

6. How do the writers explore the theme of poverty in the extract? Write two paragraphs.

   - In the first, you should comment on what the writers or the characters say about the setting or their own appearance.

   - In the second, you should comment on what Kiguunda says about the rich and poor.

Checklist for success

✔ Begin each paragraph with the point you want to make.

✔ Then include a suitable quotation (not too long) to support the point.

✔ Finish the paragraph with one or two sentences explaining the quotation or linking it to another point or piece of evidence.

✔ Use quotation marks for any direct quotation from the playscript.

Key term

rhetorical question: a question that is used to make people think, rather than requiring an answer

Reflecting on your work

7 Compare your own response to Question 6 to the two responses below. Using the comments, identify ways in which your own response could be improved and rewrite it, if needed.

Response 1

The writers show how poor the family are. They have rags and are in tatters which is a costume description by the writers which means you can see how poor they are on stage. They wear the same things each day.

Also, the hut is small. Clearly they all live together in the one room. If they had more money they could have something like Mr Kioi probably has.

— Clear opening point on the theme.

Appropriate evidence but needs quotation marks for direct quotation.

Tries to develop explanation – but rather basic.

Explanation but no direct reference to script.

Comment on Response 1

There are two paragraphs and the points are well made, but there is no use of quotation marks to show direct quotations from the script. In addition, the second paragraph, while correct, is not supported by any evidence from the playscript itself.

Response 2

The writers show the poverty of Kiguunda and Wangeci through the stage and set design. These refer to the 'one-roomed house' and the 'fading ochre', which suggests they cannot afford a bigger home or to decorate it. The fact that Gathoni sleeps on the floor and has 'rags' for a bed adds to the picture of poverty.

The second way their poverty is shown is that Kiguunda and Wangeci are aware of the difference between Mr Kioi and his wife's lives and their own. Kiguunda clearly resents the wealth of Mr Kioi, stating, 'Where would the likes of Kioi and his wife now be?' without the hard work of others.

General introductory sentence sets up points to come.

Well-chosen quotations.

Concise explanation.

Further support for main point.

Good understanding, introducing new point.

Fluently expressed point and use of evidence.

Comment on Response 2

This is a successful that which discusses two aspects of the writers' approach: set and speech. The quotations are well chosen and the two paragraphs are fluently expressed.

What you have achieved

Reading

- You have learned how to comment on characters in plays using well-chosen adjectives that match the evidence in the scene.

- You have learned how to trace themes through techniques like set design, speech and movement.

- You have learned how specific language techniques, such as rhetorical questions, can add to characterisation or how relationships are presented.

Writing

- You have learned how to construct clear paragraphs about the themes of plays which use the best-selected quotation.

- You have learned how to structure key points in more than one paragraph to make a longer response.

- You have learned appropriate vocabulary to use in your response, check for its spelling and to proofread your longer responses, avoiding the comma splice.

Speaking and listening

- You have learned how adapting tone and voice can change the way a character or relationship is viewed.

- You have learned how to bring together ideas from more than one source and then build ideas within a group.

- You have learned how to make useful judgements about your own spoken performance and that of others to aid progress.

Next steps

Reading
Conflict is a key theme in many plays. One of the most famous is *Romeo and Juliet*. Check the plot of it, or read the whole play and see how many types of conflict you can identify and who the conflict is between.

Writing
Reread the scenes between Riad and his father in Units 5.4 and 5.5. What do you think will happen next in the play? What scenes might have already happened? You could use this structure and create a complete play.

Scene 1: Riad's house. Evening. He confronts Aziz about his laziness. Aziz laughs at him.

Scene 2: Market stall. Riad argues with his dad – storms off.

Scene 3: Back at the house, Riad tells Aziz he is not covering for him anymore…

Scene 4: ....

Speaking and listening
Listen to an audio drama or listen to a short section of a film or TV drama with your eyes closed. Note down what you notice about the different voices and tones used by different characters. Can you easily tell who is who? How?

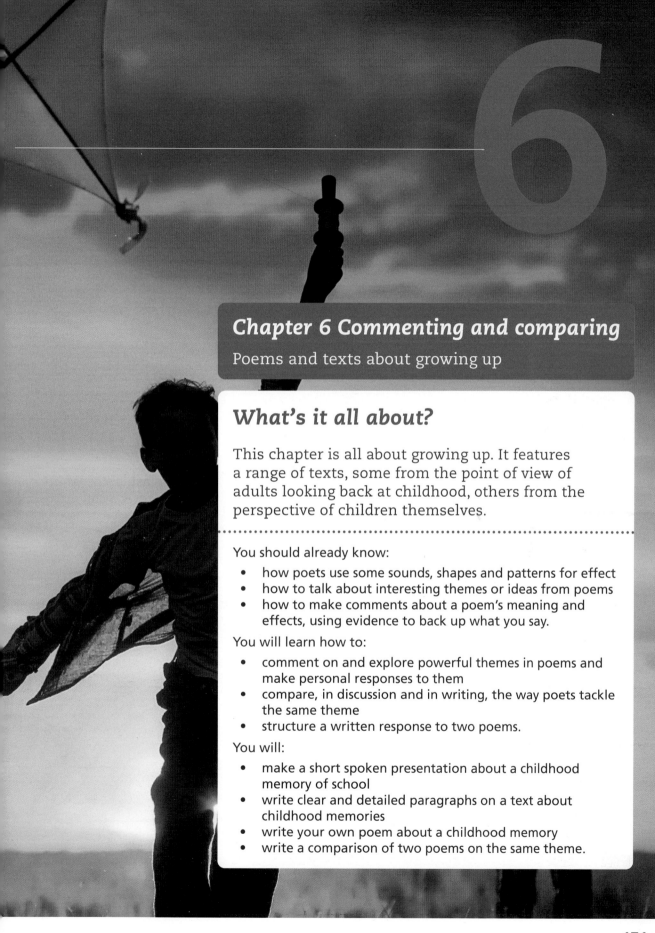

Chapter 6 Commenting and comparing
Poems and texts about growing up

What's it all about?

This chapter is all about growing up. It features a range of texts, some from the point of view of adults looking back at childhood, others from the perspective of children themselves.

You should already know:
- how poets use some sounds, shapes and patterns for effect
- how to talk about interesting themes or ideas from poems
- how to make comments about a poem's meaning and effects, using evidence to back up what you say.

You will learn how to:
- comment on and explore powerful themes in poems and make personal responses to them
- compare, in discussion and in writing, the way poets tackle the same theme
- structure a written response to two poems.

You will:
- make a short spoken presentation about a childhood memory of school
- write clear and detailed paragraphs on a text about childhood memories
- write your own poem about a childhood memory
- write a comparison of two poems on the same theme.

Enjoy reading

You will learn how to:
- explore the main ideas in a poem about childhood
- discuss your first impressions of the poem.

You are going to read a poem called 'Tich Miller', which is set in school.

1 Think about the title of the poem.

a) The poem's title is the name of a girl the poet knew at school. 'Tich' sounds like the informal word 'titch' in English. What do you think it means? Do you think it's the girl's real name? Why/why not?

b) Have you read any other poems about childhood or growing up?

2 Read the poem slowly, noting down any words or phrases you do not know.

Tich Miller

Tich Miller wore glasses
with **elastoplast**-pink frames
and had one foot three sizes larger than the other.

When they picked teams for outdoor games
she and I were always the last two
left standing by the wire-mesh fence.

We avoided one another's eyes,
stooping, perhaps, to re-tie a shoelace,
or affecting interest in the flight

of some fortunate bird, and pretended
not to hear the urgent conference:
'Have Tubby!' 'No, no, have Tich!'

Usually they chose me, the lesser dud,
and she lolloped, unselected,
to the back of the other team.

At eleven we went to different schools.
In time, I learned to get my own back,
sneering at hockey-players who couldn't spell.

Tich died when she was twelve.

By Wendy Cope

Vocabulary

elastoplast: a strip which you stick over a cut

3 Now choose five of the words or phrases you noted down. Can you work out what each one means?

a) What sort of word is it: a verb, adjective, adverb or noun?

b) Does it contain a prefix or suffix you know already? (For example, 'im' is a prefix meaning 'not'.)

c) Does the context help? Look at the rest of the sentence – what is happening?

4 Note down answers to the following big five questions.

a) **Who** is this poem about? Who is speaking?

b) **What** happens in the poem? What school activity or subject is being described? Does this kind of 'choosing' happen in your school?

c) **When** are the events happening: now, in the past or in the future?

d) **Where** do the events take place?

e) **Why** has the writer written this poem? Is she exploring a particular theme or idea? If so, what might it be?

5 What did you enjoy or find interesting about the poem? Write a sentence or two explaining how it made you feel or what it made you think about.

6 Have you ever read a poem like this before? Is it the kind of poem you would normally read?

7 Did this poem make you want to read more of Wendy Cope's work? Why? Why not?

Tracing how a narrator's views develop

You will learn how to:
- comment effectively on particular elements of a text
- use quotations to show the development of ideas.

When you comment on a text, you look at ideas and experiences in detail. However, commentary is not just about individual elements of the text, you also need to consider how these parts are linked and developed into an overall viewpoint.

Explore

Have you ever had an experience when you believed powerfully that you were in the right even when you were told you were wrong?

Read the following extract from a book written in 1913. It is the **narrator's** first day at school. The teacher has approached her to check her spelling.

> I'm sure she made me **spell after a pencil point**, like a baby, on purpose to shame me, because I was two years behind the others who were near my age. As I repeated the line Miss Amelia thought she saw her chance. She sprang to her feet, tripped a few steps toward the centre of the platform, and cried: 'Classes, attention! Our Youngest Pupil has just completed her first sentence. This sentence contains a Thought. It is a wonderfully beautiful Thought. A Thought that suggests a great moral lesson for each of us. "Birrrds – in their little nests – agreeee."'
>
> Never have I heard cooing sweetness to equal the melting tones in which Miss Amelia drawled those words. Then she continued, after a good long pause in order to give us time to allow the 'Thought' to sink in: 'There is a lesson in this for all of us. We are here in our schoolroom, like little birds in their nest. Now how charming it would be if all of us would follow the example of the birds, and at our work, and in our play, agreeee – be kind, loving, and considerate of each other. Let us all remember always this wonderful truth: "Birrrds – in their little nests – agreeee."'

Key term

narrator: the person telling the story or recounting what happened

Vocabulary

spell after a pencil point: trace a spelling in pencil over and over again and then say it out loud

upset me: knocked me over

In three steps I laid hold of her apron. Only last night Leon [my brother] had said it would come, yet whoever would have thought that I'd get a chance like this, so soon.

'Ho but they don't!' I cried. 'They fight like anything! Every day they make the feathers fly!'

In a backward stroke Miss Amelia's fingers, big and bony, struck my cheek a blow that nearly **upset me**. A red wave crossed her face, and her eyes snapped. I never had been so surprised in all my life. I was only going to tell her the truth. What she had said was altogether false. Ever since I could remember I had watched courting male birds fight all over the farm.

From *Laddie* by Gene Stratton-Porter

1   What is the narrator having to do as the extract opens?

2   What is Miss Amelia's reason for standing up to speak?

    a)   Write one phrase to explain this in your own words.

    b)   Note down one quotation from the passage to support your answer.

3   What happens after Miss Amelia has spoken? What does the narrator do and say?

4   How does the narrator behave in a way which could be seen as unacceptable?

You can trace how the narrator feels and how she responds to Miss Amelia by following what happens. This will allow you to get an overall idea of the narrator's view on the situation.

5 Copy and complete this table, filling in any missing evidence from the text.

What happens	How it is described	How the narrator feels
Paragraph 1: Miss Amelia makes her trace words and spell them out loud.	'like a baby, on purpose to shame me'	embarrassed
Paragraph 1: Teacher stops and speaks to the class.	'she saw her chance'	picked on
Paragraph 1/2: Teacher repeats the line the narrator is spelling.	She speaks with…	
Paragraph 3/speech section: Narrator interrupts her.	Narrator says…	

6 How does the narrator feel in general as a result of what has happened so far?

Now think about the final paragraph. This adds a new element to how the narrator feels and thinks about the situation.

7 Write brief answers to these questions.

a) What did Miss Amelia do when the narrator spoke to her? Would this be an acceptable way for a teacher to act today?

b) What physical details does the narrator give us about Miss Amelia (look at the vocabulary and **imagery** used)?

c) What new adjectives could you use to describe Miss Amelia here? Choose suitable words from the word bank below and find evidence from the extract to back up your choices.

regretful	quick-tempered		violent
embarrassed	irritable	grumpy	rough
cruel	spiteful		two-faced

Key term

imagery: language intended to conjure up a vivid picture in the reader's mind

8 Using some of your ideas from Questions 4, 5 and 6, write a paragraph summing up how the narrator views Miss Amelia at the beginning and end of the extract.

Start by commenting on how the narrator makes us view Miss Amelia in a bad light right from the start.

> In the first paragraph, it is clear Miss Amelia wants to make an example of the…
>
> As the passage progresses, she is presented as…
>
> In the last part of the extract, the narrator presents an even worse picture of Miss Amelia. She does this by…

Checklist for success

✔ Use character adjectives to comment on how Miss Amelia is described at different stages of the extract.

✔ Use quotations as evidence to back up the points in your commentary.

Commenting on how poets present childhood memories

You will learn how to:
- comment on the range of ways a writer gives their viewpoint or develops themes
- make clear and concise references to the texts you have read.

Writers explore memories of childhood in different ways. In this unit, you will comment on the techniques poets use to bring past experiences to life, and how their **viewpoint** – the way they see these experiences – is conveyed to the reader.

Key term

viewpoint: the attitude or feelings a writer or character has towards people or events

Explore

 1 Do you have a powerful memory from your past? It could be happy or sad. Try to write down that memory in no more than 25 words. How easy or difficult is it to express the memory?

Many poets are skilled at capturing moments from the past. Here, poet Judith Nicholls describes a childhood experience.

The Dare

Go on, I dare you,
Come on down!

Was it *me* they called?
Pretend you haven't heard,
a voice commanded in my mind.
Walk past, walk fast
and don't look down,
don't look behind.

Come on, it's easy!

The banks were steep,
The water low
And flanked with **oozing** brown.
Easy? Walk fast
But don't look down.
Walk straight, walk on,
even risk their jeers and run...

Never go near those **dykes**,
my mother said.
No need to tell me.
I'd seen stones sucked in

Vocabulary

oozing: flowing or leaking slowly

dykes: constructed canals to drain or block seawater

cowardy: slang for 'cowardly' (lacking bravery)

and covered without trace,
gulls slide to bobbing safety,
grasses drown as water rose.
No need to tell me
to avoid the place.

She ca-a-n't, she ca-a-a-n't
Cowardy, *cowardy custard!*

There's no such word as 'can't',
my father said.
I slowed my pace.
The voice stopped,
waited as I wavered, grasping breath.
My mother's wrath? My father's scorn?
A watery death?

I hesitated, then turned back,
forced myself to see the mud below.
After all, it was a dare…
There was no choice;
I had to go.

By Judith Nicholls

2 In pairs, discuss the following questions. Find evidence for your answers.

a) What 'dare' was the poet asked to do?

b) Where are the voices telling her to do the 'dare'?

c) What would her parents say if she told them?

d) Does she do the dare or does she walk on?

Judith Nicholls presents the speaker's feelings in many different ways. One way is by using words that directly tell the reader the emotions she feels.

3 Here are some definitions of words from the poem that tell us how the poet feels. For each one, write down the word from the poem.

a) a verb meaning 'to hide real feelings'

b) a noun meaning 'unpleasant comments or cries'

c) another word for 'hesitated'

d) a noun meaning 'anger'

e) a noun meaning 'sneering' or 'mockery'

4 What initial impressions of the speaker's feelings do you get?

In addition to commenting on what you are told explicitly, you can also look at other aspects of the poem, including description, and what these details imply. For example, Judith Nicholls describes the banks of the dyke as 'steep' and 'oozing brown'.

5 'Oozing' is an **onomatopoeic** word that describes the mud on the steep sides of the bank.

  a) What picture or sound comes to mind when you hear the word?

  b) What do you think the mud is like? Is it still, moving fast or moving slowly? Thick or thin?

6 Why does the poet mention the 'stones sucked in / and covered without a trace'?

7 What can you **infer** about the poet's feelings about the dyke from these descriptions?

In order to comment effectively on the methods the poet uses to convey her memories, you need to make reference to these emotions and descriptions. For example, you could say:

> The speaker feels pressurised about doing 'the dare', so she looks for an excuse not to do it. She says, 'pretend you haven't heard'. By pretending, she hopes she can walk past without her pride being damaged. She doesn't want them to know she's scared.

— Comments on her feelings.

This quotation from the poem supports the comment and explanation.

This is an explanation of what 'pretend' might imply.

This final sentence sums up the overall emotions she feels.

8 Using the 'oozing brown' quotation, write your own commentary paragraph, using a similar structure.

Start with a **topic sentence** stating what you think the speaker feels.

> The speaker looks at the bank and…

Add a sentence in which you use and explain the quotation.

> She describes it as… which means…

Then add a third sentence, commenting on what is implied by this phrase.

> This suggests she feels that the mud is…

Finish with a summary sentence.

Key terms

onomatopoeic: when a word sounds like the thing it describes (e.g. 'whisper', 'crash')

infer: to work out what someone is implying through their choice of words

Key term

topic sentence: a sentence in a paragraph – usually at the beginning – that shows the reader the main subject of the writing

Here is another poem about childhood memories, by a poet who grew up in Singapore.

Only the Moon

When I was a child I thought
The new moon was a cradle
The full moon was granny's round face.

The new moon was a banana
The full moon was a big cake.

When I was a child
I never saw the moon
I only saw what I wanted to see.

And now I see the moon
It's the moon,
Only the moon, and nothing but the moon.

By Wong May, translated by E. Thumboo

9 Answer these questions about the poem.

a) How did the speaker feel about the moon when she was very little?

b) How does the way the speaker sees the moon change as she gets older?

c) How does the speaker seem to feel about this change? Is it absolutely clear?

10 Write two paragraphs commenting on the speaker's viewpoint in 'Only the Moon'. Focus on the speaker's changing feelings.

a) In the first paragraph, comment on how she felt as a child.

b) In the second paragraph, comment on how her viewpoint changed.

Checklist for success

✔ Use a clear structure for your paragraphs – start with a topic sentence, followed by longer sentences providing evidence and commentary.

✔ End with a summary sentence.

Comparing poems on a similar topic

You will learn how to:
- draw out the key features and viewpoints in two poems and compare and contrast them
- write about these similarities and differences in a clear way.

When you compare two poems on a similar theme, you need to comment on a number of different aspects, such as the viewpoint of the two poets and the methods they use to get these viewpoints across.

Explore

In Unit 6.3, you read two poems that dealt with childhood, 'The Dare' and 'Only the Moon'. In writing a comparison, it is useful to use a simple structure to organise your ideas.

For example:

1: Introduction to the poems – who they are about, and the two experiences that are described.

2: What is similar about the poems: voice/viewpoint; form/structure; language.

3: What is different about the poems: voice/viewpoint; form/structure; language.

4: Conclusion: summing up.

1 Use this table to help you record ideas for your comparison.

    a) Copy and complete it, adding as much information as you can – even into those sections where ideas are already listed.

    b) Include short quotations to support the points you are listing.

	'The Dare'	'Only the Moon'
the story the speaker tells/the key ideas		The speaker describes different ways she sees or saw the moon. Her image of the moon was influenced by the child-like world around her.
voice/viewpoint	Told in the first person ('I') – about a past event. But uses the present tense for child's thoughts at the time.	
	Speaker is unsure, ashamed, questioning what she should do ('Pretend you haven't heard')	
form/structure		One stanza. Starts with thoughts about the past: '*When* I was a child' but changes when…
language	Description of the dyke and the bank 'Oozing brown'.	Uses metaphors…
	Other people's voices – parents, other children…	
anything else you notice about the poems	The reader doesn't know if the girl succeeded or fell down.	

2 Look at your table of notes.

a) Highlight, in one colour, anything that the two poems have in common. Don't ignore obvious similarities (for example, both poems are about children).

b) Everything that is left should be the differences. Check these again, with the poems to hand, to confirm these really are different ways of presenting the memories.

c) Check you have included evidence in the form of short quotations, where needed.

3 Share your notes with a partner and talk about the similarities and differences together.

As you do so, be precise about the parts of the poem you are referring to. For example: 'In the *first* line/ verse', '*Towards the end* of the poem', 'The *final* couplet', 'The *opening part*'.

Use words that explain what the poet or poem is doing. For example, the poet: *explores, tackles, remembers, reflects on, considers, presents, suggests, discusses, tells, recounts.*

4 After your discussion, look again at your notes.

a) Is there anything you need to add?

b) Is there anything you now think needs amending?

Develop

There are several useful words and phrases that help you to link and compare two texts. For example:

- In the same way…
- Like…
- Both…
- Also…
- Similarly…
- Whereas…

5 Complete these sentences about the poems using one of the connective words or phrases.

a) … texts deal with memories from childhood.

b) 'The Dare' describes a memory of a particular place, … 'Only the Moon' recalls a particular sight.

c) … the speaker in 'The Dare', the speaker in 'Only the Moon' remembers how her imagination had a significant effect on her.

6 Now, write one or two sentences in which you:

- compare how the speakers use the first-person ('I') voice and create a personal tone
- use one of the connective phrases.

There are probably just as many differences as similarities between the two poems. To talk about these, you need to use words or phrases that indicate difference or exception. For example:

- *Unlike* 'The Dare', it is clear in 'Only the Moon' that the poet has some happy memories.

- 'The Dare' tackles unhappy memories. *However*, 'Only the Moon' recalls some fond ones.

- *Although* 'The Dare' is about childhood memories, it is very different from 'Only the Moon'.

Here are some other words or phrases you can use to explain differences.

| but | yet | while | in contrast | even though |
| on the one hand/on the other hand |

7 Look at these two sets of sentences. Rewrite them using suitable words or phrases from the box above.

a) Wong May recalls a happy childhood memory. Judith Nicholls remembers something that made her afraid.

b) Judith Nicholls describes her feelings at the time. Wong May explores how her perceptions developed as she got older.

8 Now write one or two sentences in which you explain the difference in the form of each poem. You could comment on:

- 'The Dare' – how it includes stanzas that build up the drama/memory of the experience.

- 'Only the Moon' – how it includes thoughts and memories on one single aspect of childhood.

Respond

9 Write a comparison of both poems, commenting on the ways the poets recall their childhood.

You can use this scaffold to help you:

Both poems explore…

One of the similarities between them is…

Another is…

The poems are different in a number of ways. For example, in 'The Dare', the poet…

In addition, in 'Only the Moon'…

In conclusion, I would say that Wong May's memories of childhood are…

While…

Checklist for success

✔ Use some of the connectives you have learned about.

✔ Include direct quotations from the poems to support what you say.

✔ Use precise language ('In the first line') and verbs which help you comment on the poems ('remembers', 'suggests', 'conveys').

Sharing childhood experiences

You will learn how to:
- use discussion to comment on and compare experiences
- simplify language to help others understand detailed points.

Discussion is a good way to help you think about your own experiences, but it can also help build your confidence in communicating.

> **Explore**

Do you remember any of your 'first days' – whether at your current school, or schools you attended when you were younger? Note down answers to these questions.

1 What can you recall?

a) Who was the first person you met or became friends with?

b) What was your first lesson – or the first lesson you remember?

c) What was your first classroom like? Who was your first teacher?

2 How did you feel? Working on your own, draw three emojis on a sticky note or small card, to show how you felt on your first day. You can use well-known emojis, or make up your own.

You are now going to talk about your experiences in a small group. Before you do, jot down what speaking skills will help you engage and interest your group in what you say. For example:

- *Make eye contact.*

3 Add your own list of top tips.

4 Now, using your own emojis and the notes you made as a prompt, talk for one minute to the rest of the group about your experiences and memories of your first day.

5 Once you have finished speaking, the rest of the group should try to think of one question each to ask you. For example: 'Who was the first friend you made?'

6 Was there anything your listeners didn't understand? Could you have said anything more simply?

Develop

It is challenging to have to speak on your own about a topic, but sharing ideas can be fun and interesting. However, it is important that you speak clearly and listen carefully.

Your group is now going to discuss the following topic:

'Schools should do more to help new students on their first day.' To what extent do you agree or disagree with this statement?

7 Before your discussion, spend a few minutes thinking about your own views on this and how you could support your view. Note down:

My view: [disagree strongly][disagree a little][agree a little][agree strongly]
My main point:
My second point:

8 Now, discuss the topic.

- Allocate roles such as chairperson and scribe if you think it will help the discussion.

- Listen carefully to what everyone says and ask questions where needed to draw out other people's ideas.

- Make sure everyone gets a chance to contribute. For example, use questions such as 'So, Shahid, what did you think?' or 'Does anyone have something else to add before we move on?'

- If you are not clear about something, ask them politely to explain again, or check what they mean. For example, 'So what you're saying is…'.

- Check each point is discussed fully: don't move on too quickly to another point.

Respond

9 Once you have finished, think about your own contribution and that of the rest of the group. Write a brief evaluation with these headings.

- What I did well/not so well

- How the group did: what went well in the discussion/what didn't go so well

Writing your own poem about childhood

You will learn how to:

- draft ideas for your poem and spend time shaping and improving it
- present your poem to others and evaluate its effect and impact.

You have talked and read about your own and others' childhood memories in this chapter. Now you will have the chance to turn one of your own memories into a poem.

Explore

1 Start by thinking of a possible idea of a childhood memory to write about. It could be related to one of the following:

- a person in your family you love or admire, for example, a memory of being with them
- a particular place: this could be a park, a friend's house or bedroom, a beach, a tree you used to climb
- an event or experience that made an impression on you: a first day at school, a birthday party, moving into a new house.

2 Poems about memories often work best when they include vivid descriptions. Once you have chosen the memory, try to place yourself in that moment. Copy and complete the diagram below.

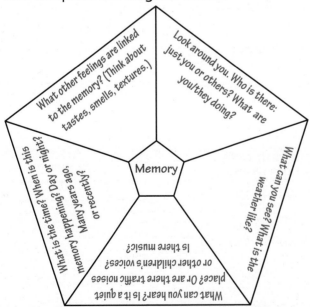

Diagram segments:
- Look around you. Who is there: just you or others? What are you/they doing?
- What can you see? What is the weather like?
- What can you hear? Is it a quiet place? Or are there traffic noises or other children's voices? Is there music?
- What is the time? When is this memory happening? Day or night? Many years ago, or recently?
- What other feelings are linked to the memory? (Think about tastes, smells, textures.)
- Memory

Develop

Now is the time to shape your ideas into a specific form. Here is one suggestion you could follow:

Form

- told in first person ('I')

- two verses – each of four lines

- first verse: each line begins 'I remember…' (this is the memory)

- second verse: each line begins 'Now, I…' (this is the same person now – life has changed).

Alternatives

- You could try writing a sonnet, although you will need to remind yourself of the sonnet form (see Stage 7, Chapter 6).

- Or write a unique poem, with its own shape and layout.

3 Write your first draft.

Checklist for success

✔ Choose a shape or layout.

✔ Decide on the voice ('I', 'she', 'he', 'you').

✔ Think about how you might use techniques such as **assonance**, **alliteration** and onomatopoeia.

✔ Consider rhyme – how might it help or hinder the poem?

✔ Cut out unnecessary, weak words or phrases ('nice', 'really') or articles you don't need ('the', 'a', 'some').

Respond

4 Share your draft poem with someone else. Evaluate the success of their poem by:

   a) selecting words, phrases and lines that make a strong impression

   b) identifying clear feelings or emotions conveyed

   c) noting the effect of any techniques.

Make a note of anything that you didn't think worked so well, and then hand the draft back.

5 Redraft your poem in the light of the comments, adding new or better ideas.

Key terms

assonance: use of similar or identical vowel sounds in groups of words (e.g. 'the hooded man in the woods')

alliteration: the same letter or sound at the start of a group of words (e.g. 'the lovely lark's lilting song')

Responding to two poems on the same theme

You will learn how to:
- write about the similarities and differences between two poems.

You are going to comment on how two poems explore a similar theme, using the understanding you have built up in this chapter.

Reread 'Tich Miller' from Unit 6.1 and the poem below.

Partners

Find a partner,
says sir, and sit
with him or her.
A whisper here,
a shuffle there,
a rush of feet.
One pair,
another pair,
till twenty four
sit safely on the floor
and all are gone
but one
who stands,
like stone,
and waits;
tall,
still,

alone.

By Judith Nicholls

Understanding the poems

1 Check your basic understanding of both poems by answering these questions.

   a) Where do both poems take place? Which details tell you this?

   b) Who isn't chosen in each poem? Do we know?

   c) How are the classes being divided in the poems? Is it in the same way? How do you know?

2 Look at 'Tich Miller'. Decide which statements apply to the speaker and which to Tich.

	Tich	The speaker
wears pink-framed glasses		
dies, aged twelve		
is nicknamed 'Tubby'		
usually chosen before the other one		

Thinking about the poems' purposes and features

3 Look again at both poems. Copy and complete the grid, ticking the correct column and adding a reference or line number to support your answer.

Feature	'Partners'	'Tich Miller'
told in the first person		
short single- or two-word lines		
includes spoken language		
uses occasional rhyme		
uses the present tense		
uses the past tense		
ends with a line that gives new information		

Looking at the poems in detail

4 In 'Partners' the child who is left without a partner stands 'like stone'. Why do you think the poet uses this **simile**?

5 In what way does the form of 'Partners' reflect the story it tells? Write a sentence explaining your ideas.

6 In 'Tich Miller', there are two clues in the first half of the poem that Tich has some form of disability. What words or phrases suggest this?

7 Why does the poet mention the 'fortunate bird'? What is she suggesting by using this image?

8 The poet uses a two-word phrase to suggest she is not as bad at sports as Tich (as far as the other pupils are concerned). What is the phrase?

9 What evidence is there in 'Tich Miller' that the speaker is looking back at her childhood and schooldays?

Key term

....

simile: a comparison between two things that uses the words 'as' or 'like' (e.g. 'Our garden is like a jungle')

10 Copy and complete the grid to help you explore the similarities and differences in the poems. Some ideas have already been added.

Feature	'Partners'	'Tich Miller'
What is the situation that is being described?		Outdoor 'games' (sports) at school, when teams are chosen one by one from the whole class.
Whose point of view is it in the poem? How can you tell?		The poet is speaking in the first person ('I') about a particular event happening to her.
When is the situation or story happening? (Now? In the past? Both?)		
How does the structure and layout of the poem add to its effect?	The last three words are on their own, like the poet, and are also thin and tall to look at.	
What distinctive uses of language are there, and what is their effect?		'she lolloped, unselected' – tells us Tich wasn't chosen at all, and how her disability made her move.

11 Now write three paragraphs about the two poems, comparing and contrasting them.

a) In the first paragraph, compare the stories each poem tells and explain who is telling them.

b) In the second paragraph, compare the viewpoints and the message, if there is one (for example, school life is horrible). Make sure you refer to the language used.

c) In the third paragraph, compare the structure and layout and how this affects the viewpoint given.

12 Compare your own response to Question 12 to the two opening paragraphs below. The two openings tackle the first aspect in the table. Once you have read them, identify ways in which your own response could be improved. Rewrite it, if needed.

Response 1

'Partners' is about how the poet is chosen last when the class splits into pairs. The poem 'Tich Miller' shows how the poet and another girl are the last to be chosen for sports games outdoors. The poets express how **ashamed and how unhappy** they are about the situation but can't do anything about it. It is worse for Tich because she is actually the last, 'usually they chose me', and she is disabled which isn't fair.

— Explains the 'stories' each poem tells.

— Two accurate adjectives are used to describe the poets' feelings.

— The last sentence begins to explore a point of contrast and includes a suitable quotation.

Comment on Response 1

The contents of both poems are neatly introduced, but the sentences could be linked to show whether or not they are similar, using connective words such as 'both' or 'whereas'. The subtle differences between how the two poets feel – or felt – needs more attention, as does the comment on Tich herself. The quotation is well-chosen.

 13 Now read this next response. In what ways is it better?

Response 2

Both poems deal with sad childhood memories, for example, when you are looking for a partner in class, or waiting to be chosen in team sports, when you are 'always the last'. The poem 'Partners' doesn't say that it is the poet who is left alone, as it is just 'one who stands [...] alone', but it basically tells the same story as 'Tich Miller'. However, one big difference is that the focus is on two children in 'Tich Miller', the poet and Tich, and just on one child in 'Partners'. The narrator in 'Tich Miller' feels ashamed, but unlike 'Partners' is not the very last person left as **Tich isn't chosen at all**.

— Linking word draws comparisons.

— Suitable quotation supports point about the poems' stories.

— Explains a key difference between the two poems.

— Explains another difference in the story.

Comment on Response 2

This explains in some detail the similarities and differences between the two poems and their stories. It could perhaps have dealt with Tich's disability and said something about how the account changes towards the end, but this is clear and uses some appropriate supporting evidence. Connective words and phrases are generally helpful.

What you have achieved

Reading

- You have been able to identify key techniques poets use.
- You have commented on the themes and ideas in a range of poems.
- You have compared and contrasted the ways poets tackle similar themes.

Writing

- You have been able to structure an effective comparison of two poems.
- You have been able to link ideas together so that your points are clear.
- You have combined a range of poetic techniques to write your own poem.

Speaking and listening

- You have taken part in group discussions in order to express your views on poems.
- You have used talk to think again about your ideas and amend them if needed.
- You have developed verbal and non-verbal techniques to make your points.

Next steps

Reading

Several of the poets in this chapter have written other poems about childhood. Find out more about Judith Nicholls and Wendy Cope. Have they written other poems on similar themes?

Create your own mini-anthology of poems about childhood. You could copy or stick them into an exercise book with suitable drawings or photos. Try to find a mix of funny and sad poems which reflect the different memories poets have of childhood.

Find any two poems on a similar theme. Create a poster divided into three columns. In the first and third columns note down anything specific to each poem. In the middle column, note down anything they have in common.

Writing

Write a poem about childhood that uses the shape or layout to reflect what is happening or the feelings conveyed. For example, you could create a poem about a tennis game with words on either side of the page to reflect the shots back and forth over the net; or you could create a poem in the shape of a birthday cake with memories of a birthday (yours or someone else's).

Speaking and listening

Find a poem or poems that would be suitable for reading aloud to a younger child. Why would it be effective? Practise a reading of it, adapting how you speak and using gestures to make it appeal to your audience.

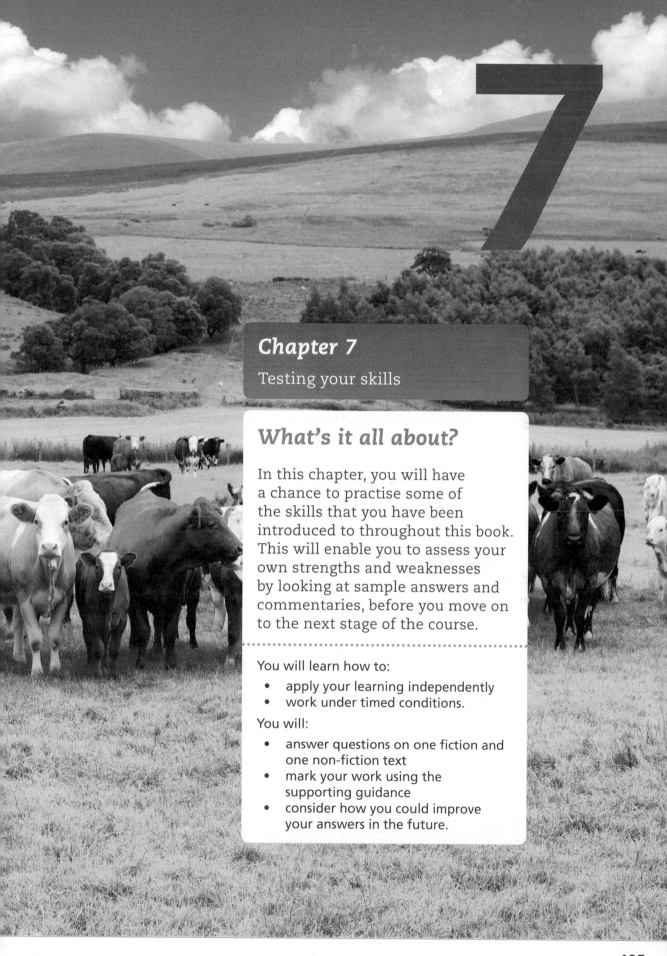

Chapter 7
Testing your skills

What's it all about?

In this chapter, you will have a chance to practise some of the skills that you have been introduced to throughout this book. This will enable you to assess your own strengths and weaknesses by looking at sample answers and commentaries, before you move on to the next stage of the course.

You will learn how to:
- apply your learning independently
- work under timed conditions.

You will:
- answer questions on one fiction and one non-fiction text
- mark your work using the supporting guidance
- consider how you could improve your answers in the future.

Reading and writing questions on non-fiction texts

Task 1: Reading

Read the extract from an information text on foot and mouth disease. Then answer the questions.

Foot and mouth disease is a viral infection that can affect a wide range of animals. These include cattle, sheep, goats, hedgehogs, rats, deer and some zoo animals.

The virus is highly **infectious** and spreads easily 5 through direct contact with infected animals or by airborne droplets. Wind can carry the virus particles very long distances – possibly 100 miles or more.

The infected animal develops a fever and then blisters, mainly in the mouth or on the feet. General symptoms 10 include going off their feed and lameness. Cattle show a reduction in milk **yield** and may develop longer-lasting ill health such as heart disease and **sterility**.

The infection does not usually prove fatal to animals, except perhaps in the case of the very young. The 15 animals are **slaughtered** to control the disease and stop it spreading through livestock. There is no cure for foot and mouth disease and it is very infectious.

Animals can get the disease by coming into contact with anything that has been contaminated by the 20 virus such as dung, feed, trucks, loading ramps, farmers' boots, and even paths and roads. This is why movement restrictions are put in place once foot and mouth is found.

If foot and mouth disease became widespread around 25 the world, it would cause economic problems for farmers and welfare problems for the animals. The UK outbreak in 2001 resulted in around seven million animals being slaughtered. However, time is running out. The World Organisation for Animal Health says 30 that the disease is now endemic in several parts of Asia and in most of Africa and the Middle East.

Vocabulary

infectious: easily spread to other creatures

yield: the amount produced

sterility: a condition that means they cannot have calves

slaughtered: killed in large numbers

1 Which two of the following statements about foot and mouth disease are correct? (2)

   a) Foot and mouth is a disease that harms domestic pets.

   b) This is a very serious disease.

   c) This disease only spreads through the air.

   d) It is easy to tell if an animal has this disease.

2 Find an adjective in paragraph 1 which shows that many species are affected by the disease. (1)

3 Which of these words from the first paragraph has a prefix? (1)

   a) disease   **b)** infection   **c)** include.

4 Write one phrase which suggests that foot and mouth is easy to catch. (1)

5 Why has the writer used a dash in line 8? (1)

6 Find a word in line 8 which means that cattle suffering from foot and mouth produce less milk than healthy ones. (1)

7 Note down three ways in which foot and mouth can be spread. (2)

8 Write a suitable heading for paragraph 3. (2)

9 Read the first sentence of paragraph 4. What does it tell the reader? (1)

   a) The virus usually kills young animals.

   b) The virus is not fatal.

   c) You would not expect the virus to kill animals but it sometimes does.

10 Combine these two sentences into a single sentence using a connective that clarifies the relationship between the two. (1)

> Animals can get the disease by coming into contact with anything that has been contaminated by the virus such as dung, feed, trucks, loading ramps, farmers' boots, and even paths and roads. This is why movement restrictions are put in place once foot and mouth is found.

Total (13)

Read this text based on an extract from a website about controlling diseases. Then answer the questions.

The process of quarantine separates and limits the movement of animals, people or in some cases plants; it is a 'state of **compulsory** isolation'. This is often to help prevent the spread of illness and disease, such as where a person may have been exposed to an infectious disease. 5 Quarantine can be enforced as part of border control as well as within a nation's boundaries.

The word itself comes from *quaranta* (seventeenth-century Italian). It means 'forty', which is the number of days that ships had to be isolated before the crew or anyone 10 aboard could go ashore during **outbreaks** of the Black Death – a form of plague. This made sure that they were not infected with the plague before they went into a new country that did not have anyone with the illness.

Some human illnesses still exist that spread very easily, 15 so doctors advise us not to mix with others and to wash everything that we use very thoroughly if we fall ill with them.

Perhaps the strictest quarantine rules in the world apply in Australia. Because Australia is near to Southeast Asia 20 and the Pacific, which have many pests and diseases, quarantine in northern Australia is extremely important. If goods or plants are brought into the country with pests and diseases, it would damage the ecosystem and be very costly to local farms and agricultural businesses. 25

In some countries, there are also plants that are considered to be harmful, usually because they grow quickly and overgrow everything in their path. If you find these plants on your land, you will be asked to take steps to stop them from spreading and you may even have to report it to the 30 government.

In the United Kingdom, to reduce the risk of introducing rabies from continental Europe, dogs – and most other animals introduced to the country – used to have to spend six months in quarantine at an HM Customs and 35 Excise pound.

This process was abolished in 2000 and, instead, a scheme known as Pet Passports was introduced, where animals can avoid quarantine if they have documentation – a 'passport' – showing they are up to date with all their 40 **vaccinations**.

Vocabulary

compulsory: something that must be done

outbreaks: when lots of people get a disease at the same time

vaccinations: injections that prevent animals or people getting a disease

11 According to the extract, quarantine is: (1)

    a) the number of days you had to stay away from someone who had the plague in the 1600s

    b) a word to describe keeping sick people and healthy people apart

    c) a way to keep people or animals away from others.

12 Find a phrase in paragraph 1 which shows that the writer is giving examples to make their meaning clear. (1)

13 Explain in your own words what the writer means by 'damage the ecosystem seriously' in paragraph 4. (2)

14 Does an animal have to go into quarantine to enter the United Kingdom? (2)

15 Write a summary of 70–90 words explaining why quarantine is important. (5)

16 Select one feature which suggests to you that this extract is from a text that aims to explain. (1)

Total (12)

Task 2: Writing

Write an article for young children that gives information about a minor childhood illness.

You will need to:

- choose an illness that you know about or invent one
- use headings to help make the information clear – for example, first signs that you have caught it, how it is caught, how to treat it.

Do not include illustrations.

Write your plan out first.

Total (25)

Reading and writing questions on fiction texts

Task 3: Reading

Read this passage from *Out of the Ashes* by Michael Morpurgo. It is about a girl called Becky who lives on a farm where the animals have caught foot and mouth disease. They have to be destroyed to stop the disease spreading to other farms.

Thursday, March 15th

Our farm isn't ours any more. People I don't even know come and go everywhere. They're all over the place, like ants. There's been lorries coming in and out all day, bringing in railway sleepers and straw for the fire. And there's diggers, two of them, digging the 5 **trench** in Front Field. I can see them now from my window, waving their arms about like great yellow monsters, doing a hideous dance of death to the thunderous music of their engines.

The phone rings all the time now, but we don't pick 10 it up and we don't answer messages unless we have to. Auntie Liz left a message, so did Jay, so did Gran, all saying how terrible it is, how sorry they are, how they're thinking of us. Auntie Liz was in tears, and Jay says it was horrible of her to have quarrelled with me 15 like she did that day. (I'd forgotten all about it long ago) and she said how much she misses me. I miss her too – lots. Gran says she wishes she could be with us, to help us. But I'm glad she's not. Three of us being silent, being so full of sadness is enough. She'd only 20 make it worse. Besides, we can manage on our own.

Mum sent me to the end of the lane to pick up the post and the milk this morning. The policeman was still there, still smoking. He said he was sorry too. Then he gave me a bit of a talking-to. I don't remember much 25 of what he said, something about a light at the end of the tunnel. He was trying to be nice. And I could see he was upset for us, really upset, not pretending.

Vocabulary

trench: a deep ditch

Mum says it's the first time since she's been married that she's ever had to buy milk. [...] 30

Most of the day, Dad sits at his desk smoking and saying nothing. There's no work for him to do any more. No milking. No feeding the animals. No cheesemaking. He hasn't been back into his cheese store to check the cheese. I don't think he can bear to look at them. 35

From *Out of the Ashes* by Michael Morpurgo

Now answer the following questions.

1 What type of writing is this? (2)

2 How do you know? (2)

3 Explain one way in which the opening sentence tries to gain the reader's attention. (1)

4 Which of the following statements best sums up what this extract is about? (1)

a) It is about a girl who lives on a farm.

b) It is about a typical morning on a farm.

c) It is about a difficult time for a family and their farm.

5 Read the following two sentences from the passage. Why is this an effective comparison? (1)

> People I don't even know come and go everywhere. They're all over the place, like ants.

6 What do the words 'like great yellow monsters' suggest about the girl's feelings about the diggers? (1)

7 Explain in your own words the meaning of each of the following, as it is used in the text: (2)

   a) hideous (line 8)

   b) thunderous (line 9).

8 The writer uses brackets in paragraph 2, when describing Jay's message. Why do you think the writer uses the brackets here? (1)

9 Which phrase in paragraph 2 tells us how upset Becky and her parents are? (1)

10 Read the final sentence of paragraph 2. In your own words, sum up what kind of girl you think Becky is. (2)

11 Why does the writer use the phrase 'really upset' in the sentence 'And I can see he was upset for us, really upset, not pretending' at the end of paragraph 3? (1)

12 Read the final paragraph. In your own words, describe how the writer uses sentence length and structure to describe Becky's father. (2)

13 Using information from the whole extract, explain in your own words how Becky's parents must be feeling. Use quotations to support your points. (5)

14 The passage creates an atmosphere of unease, as so many things are not as they would normally be for the family. Explain how the writer has done this, using examples from the passage. (3)

Total (25)

Task 4: Writing

In the passage you have read, Becky's day was not at all as she would normally expect.

Write a story of your own in the first person about a day when things do not go as expected.

You will need to consider:

- **character:** are there any other characters?

- **setting:** where do things happen unexpectedly?

- **plot:** why do things happen this way? What do you do/ feel?

- **structure:** does your story have a beginning, a middle and an end?

Total (25)

Assessing your progress: Reading and writing non-fiction

In this section, you are going to look at your answers and some suggestions about what you could have written. You can use these suggestions to assess your strengths and weaknesses and to practise improving your answers.

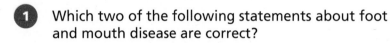

Task 1: Reading

1 Which two of the following statements about foot and mouth disease are correct?

    a) Foot and mouth is a disease that harms domestic pets.

    b) This is a very serious disease.

    c) This disease only spreads through the air.

    d) It is easy to tell if an animal has this disease.

Answer: b) and d) (1 mark for each correct choice, up to 2 marks)

Where might you have gone wrong?

If you chose a) you may have seen the word 'rats' and thought that some people keep them as pets. However, the list includes several wild and even exotic animals and no other animals commonly kept as pets, so the statement is not precise enough to be a correct answer.

If you chose c) you may have read the word 'airborne' so thought that the statement is true. However, the disease also spreads by direct contact, so saying that it *only* spreads through air is incorrect.

2 Find an adjective in paragraph 1 which shows that many species are affected by the disease.

Answer: 'wide' (1)

Where might you have gone wrong?

You may not have remembered what an adjective is. However, you can sometimes find a word without knowing what type it is. The question asked you to find a word that meant 'more than one', so look for a word that suggests quantity. Both 'wide' and 'range' can suggest an amount of something, which would have helped you to narrow down your search.

3 Which of these words from the first paragraph has a prefix?

    a) disease

    b) infection

    c) include.

Answer: 'include' (1)

Where might you have gone wrong?

You may not have remembered what a prefix is. If so, look back through the book to revise word types.

4 Write one phrase which suggests that foot and mouth is easy to catch.

Answer: 'highly infectious' (1 mark)

Where might you have gone wrong?

You may have thought that 'spreads easily' or 'long distances' were acceptable phrases as they describe the way the disease can travel. However, the answer asks about how easy it is to catch and 'highly infectious' suggests this more explicitly.

5   Why has the writer used a dash in line 8?

Answer: to show that what follows is an example/extra information

Where might you have gone wrong?

You may not have remembered why dashes are used. But you could have worked it out as you know that punctuation usually suggests a relationship between pieces of information.

6   Find a word in line 8 which means that cattle suffering from foot and mouth produce less milk than healthy ones.

Answer: 'reduction' (1)

Where might you have gone wrong?

You may not have known what 'reduction' means. Remember, you can often find a clue to a word's meaning if you break it up into parts or think of other similar words. In this case 'reduction' is like 'reduce', which means 'to make smaller'. Also, the prefix 're' is often used in words to suggest a backward movement or lessening of something.

7 Note down three ways in which foot and mouth can be spread.

Answer: *coming into contact with a source of infection; coming into contact with dung/feed/trucks/loading ramps/farmer's boots/paths/roads; virus droplets in the air (1 mark if one or two correct answers and 2 marks if three correct answers)*

Where might you have gone wrong?

You might have read the question and remembered that there are two ways that the disease spreads – air and contact – and thought that this was the answer. However, paragraph 5 gives more specific details about ways in which the disease is spread.

 8 Write a suitable heading for paragraph 3.

Answer: *Symptoms of illness/Signs of illness/Effects of foot and mouth – or any heading that accurately sums up that this paragraph is about the tangible signs of the condition (1 mark for expression of the concept of evidence and 1 mark for making a link to the illness, up to 2 marks)*

Where might you have gone wrong?

This type of question is testing whether or not you can pick out the main idea of a paragraph. In this case, it is about *ways* that people can see an animal *is ill*. You may have focused on one side of this in your heading, but a good heading would include both ideas. Make sure you pick out the main idea – ask yourself what message the writer wants to communicate.

 9 Read the first sentence of paragraph 4. What does it tell the reader?

a) The virus usually kills young animals.

b) The virus is not fatal.

c) You would not expect the virus to kill animals, but it sometimes does.

Answer: *c) You would not expect the virus to kill animals, but it sometimes does. (1)*

Where might you have gone wrong?

If you chose a) then you probably read that the virus does 'perhaps' kill the very young ones, but 'usually' means 'almost always'.

10 Combine these two sentences into a single sentence using a connective that clarifies the relationship between the two.

> Animals can get the disease by coming into contact with anything that has been contaminated by the virus such as dung, feed, trucks, loading ramps, farmers' boots, and even paths and roads. This is why movement restrictions are put in place once foot and mouth is found.

Answer: In the second sentence, 'This is why' should be replaced with a connective showing that the second sentence is a consequence of the first, for example 'therefore'. (1)

Where might you have gone wrong?

You may have written 'and', which is a conjunction but which does not suggest any relationship between the two sentences. A connective such as 'therefore' suggests that what is described in the first sentence leads to the second.

11 According to the extract, quarantine is:

a) the number of days you had to stay away from someone who had the plague in the 1600s

b) a word to describe keeping sick people and healthy people apart

c) a way to keep people or animals away from others.

Answer: c) a way to keep people or animals away from others (1)

Where might you have gone wrong?

You may have remembered that the passage tells us 'quarantine' comes from the word *quaranta*, which is the number of days someone with the plague needed to be isolated for, but this is the word's *origin*, not its meaning. You may have understood that quarantine means keeping the sick and healthy apart, but it does not just apply to humans, so b) is incorrect.

Find a phrase in paragraph 1 which shows that the writer is giving examples to make their meaning clear.

Answer: 'such as' (1)

Where might you have gone wrong?

You might be used to seeing 'e.g.' when examples are going to be given. However, there are different ways of writing this out. Sometimes authors might write 'for instance', 'for example' or 'such as'.

 Explain in your own words what the writer means by 'damage the ecosystem seriously' in paragraph 4.

Answer: 1 mark for cause a lot of harm to and 1 mark for environment/natural system

Where might you have gone wrong?

You may have only explained part of the phrase. Remember to read the question carefully and tackle everything you are asked to do.

 Does an animal have to go into quarantine to enter the United Kingdom?

Answer: no (1 mark for 'no' and 2 marks for an answer that explains that a pet passport/proof of vaccination has replaced quarantine)

Where might you have gone wrong?

You might have misread the passage and thought that Britain still uses quarantine. The key phrase in the topic sentence is 'used to', which you may have missed if you were skim reading. Make sure that you *scan* when you are looking for a key fact.

15 Write a summary of 70–90 words explaining why quarantine is important.

Answer: 1 mark for each of the following:

Mark	Answer	Further information
1	Identification of four main points.	Quarantine stops illness spreading to new countries that don't have the disease.
		It stops healthy people/plants/animals getting sick.
		It can protect countries from damage to their ecosystem.
		It saves loss of money to agricultural businesses.
		It stops fast-spreading diseases from becoming epidemics.
		It stops destructive plants from spreading.
1	Use of own words and not copying text too much.	
1	Organisation of ideas (the order and groupings of ideas that you include).	
1	Accuracy of language (your choice of grammar, spelling and punctuation).	
1	Length of 70–90 words.	

Where might you have gone wrong?

You may not have found all the points. Remember that the number of marks given is a clue to the number of points needed in your answer. You might have given lots of examples rather than sticking to the point, so you may have written about rabies or the Black Death or pet passports. You may have given additional details, such as how washing can help to reinforce quarantine.

 16 Select one feature which suggests to you that this extract is from a text that aims to explain.

Answer: 1 mark for one of the following: it starts with a term and then defines it/it gives facts and figures/it includes historical background/it gives examples

Where might you have gone wrong?

You may not have remembered the features of an information text. If so, go back to Unit 2.2.

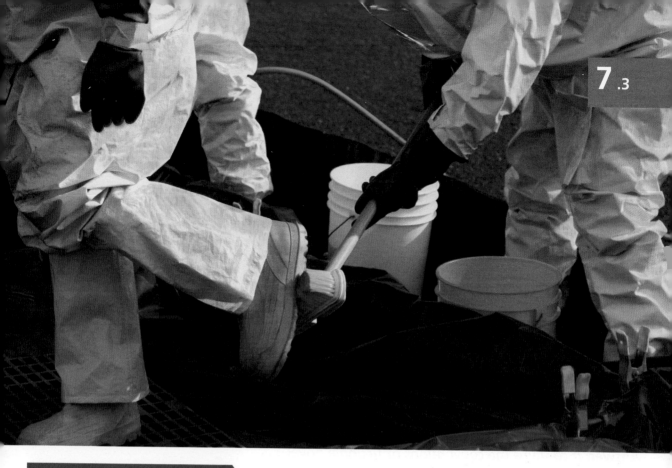

Task 2: Writing

Use the table below to self-assess your answer to questions. You may find it helpful to highlight using a different colour when you find evidence of what you have done well. Remember that your teacher will also look at your spelling, punctuation and sentence structures before you can award yourself a level.

Purpose and audience		Text structure
It is sometimes clear who you are writing for and you have used the features of an article giving information.	You have sometimes written as a journalist in your article.	You have tried to write your ideas in the form of an article giving information but end up telling the story of when you had the childhood illness or describing it in too much detail.
It is often clear who you are writing for and you have used the features of an article giving information.	You have almost always written as a journalist in your article.	Your article often follows the usual structure of an information article with a headline, subheading, introductory paragraph and then an explanation with references to facts.
It is clear who you are writing for and you have used the features of an article giving information.	You have written as a journalist all through your article.	Your article follows the usual structure of an information article with a headline, subheading, introductory paragraph and then an explanation in more detail with references to facts and evidence.

Assessing your progress: Reading and writing fiction

Task 3: Reading

 1 What type of writing is this?

Answer: fiction – a novel (1 mark for each)

Where might you have gone wrong?

You may have thought that the extract was a short story, as stories of any kind share common features. However, in this case the extract did not contain a whole **story arc** (a beginning, a middle and an end). Also, the characters and setting were not introduced as they would be at the start of a short story.

 2 How do you know?

Answer: It contains the conventions of fiction/a novel, such as: finely drawn characters; focus on events, feelings and relationships; a setting; detailed description, imagery, atmosphere; is part of a story arc; does not contain whole story arc. It does not show the conventions of non-fiction (no subheadings or other layout features). (1 mark for any of these points up to a total of 2 marks)

Where might you have gone wrong?

You may not have been able to explain your choice of writing type. If this is the case, look again at the ways that fiction and non-fiction texts can be identified.

 3 Explain one way in which the opening sentence tries to gain the reader's attention.

Answer: 1 mark for one of the following: It creates a mystery/makes us question why/sounds very alarming/life changing.

Where might you have gone wrong?

You may not have remembered that writers usually try to plant some seeds or 'hooks' in their readers' minds early on.

> **Key term**
>
> **story arc:** the full plot of a story – beginning, middle and end

4 Which of the following statements best sums up what this extract is about?

  a) It is about a girl who lives on a farm.

  b) It is about a typical morning on a farm.

  c) It is about a difficult time for a family and their farm.

Answer: c) It is about a difficult time for a family and their farm. (1)

Where might you have gone wrong?

You may have read a) and decided that as both facts that it contains are true, it was the correct choice. However, if you are asked to sum something up then you need to ensure that everything has been covered. This statement does not include the fact that something is clearly unusual and uncomfortable for Becky and her family. If you chose b) then you have missed the clues that things are not as they would normally be. To pick these up you need to read carefully and draw inferences from the text.

5 Read the following two sentences from the passage. Why is this an effective comparison?

> People I don't even know come and go everywhere. They're all over the place, like ants.

Answer: The comparison suggests quantity/a lot of movement. (1)

Where might you have gone wrong?

You may have identified *who* was being compared with *what*. It is important to read the question carefully as at this level you are expected to give more detailed explanations.

6 What do the words 'like great yellow monsters' suggest about the girl's feelings about the diggers?

Answer: They suggest that Becky finds them frightening/threatening. (1)

Where might you have gone wrong?

You might have focused on the word 'great' and said that she thinks they are big, but this is not a feeling. Their size might make her feel scared, which would be acceptable as an answer.

7 Explain in your own words the meaning of each of the following, as it is used in the text:

    a) hideous (line 8)

    b) thunderous (line 9).

Answer: 1 mark for ugly/unattractive (a) and 1 mark for loud/frightening (b)

Where might you have gone wrong?

You may not have known these words. Remember that you should read the whole sentence to try to work out the meaning from the context.

 8 The writer uses brackets in paragraph 2, when describing Jay's message. Why do you think the writer uses the brackets here?

Answer: to show that the information that they contain is not part of the meaning of the main narrative at this point (1)

Where might you have gone wrong?

You may have only noted that the text in brackets contains extra information, when the key point is that it allows Becky to show her own feelings here, in the middle of telling the reader about Jay's message.

9 Which phrase in paragraph 2 tells us how upset Becky and her parents are?

Answer: 'full of sadness' (1)

Where might you have gone wrong?

If you only wrote 'sadness' or any other part of the phrase you will not gain any marks, as the question asks for a phrase.

 10 Read the final sentence of paragraph 2. In your own words, sum up what kind of girl you think Becky is.

Answer: any of the following or similar ideas: independent, brave, strong, trusts her parents, believes in her family (1 mark for each, up to 2 marks)

Where might you have gone wrong?

Remember that the number of marks on offer is a clue to the amount that you need to write, so you need to make two points here. If you found it difficult to work out what Becky is like from the sentence, look back through the book to help you develop your inference skills.

11 Why does the writer use the phrase 'really upset' in the sentence 'And I can see he was upset for us, really upset, not pretending' at the end of paragraph 3?

Answer: to show that his feelings were genuine (1)

Where might you have gone wrong?

You may have read the word 'really' and thought that it is often used as an intensifier, so you said that it 'added emphasis' or similar. However, in this sentence the following clause is 'not pretending', which means that the other meaning of really (truly) is being used. It is important to read the whole question and to consider whether your explanation fits with it.

12 Read the final paragraph. In your own words, describe how the writer uses sentence length and structure to describe Becky's father.

Answer: a series of short, simple sentences (2)

Where might you have gone wrong?

You might have focused on what the sentences said *about* Becky's father. If so, make sure that you read the question carefully. You may not have been able to use the correct terminology for the different types of sentences. If this is the case, look back through the book to revise sentence types – see Units 1.7, 1.8 and 2.9.

13 Using information from the whole extract, explain in your own words how Becky's parents must be feeling. Use quotations to support your points.

Answer: Give 1 mark each for up to two feelings from this list:

- *taken over*
- *sad*
- *unsettled*
- *uncomfortable*
- *bored.*

Give 1 extra mark if a quotation has been used to back either point up.

Where might you have gone wrong?

You may have found it hard to work out how the parents were feeling. In order to do this, you need to be able to infer from the details given. Look back through the book to revise how to infer meaning from a text – see Units 1.2 and 1.3.

You might have forgotten to add evidence from the extract, which will limit the marks you can get for the question. Remember to look for key words in the questions and keep them in mind as you write.

14 The passage creates an atmosphere of unease as so many things are not as they would normally be for the family. Explain how the writer has done this using examples from the passage.

Answer: Give 1 mark each for up to two examples from this list:

- people they don't know are everywhere
- phone rings all the time
- can't see family members
- have to buy milk
- policeman at gate
- Dad not working

Give 1 extra mark if a quotation or reasoning has been used to back either point up.

Where might you have gone wrong?

You may have forgotten that when you are asked to explain you must add evidence and/or reasoning.

Use the table below to assess your answer to this question. You may find it helpful to highlight using a different colour when you find evidence of what you have done well. Remember that your teacher will also look at your spelling, punctuation and sentence structures before you can award yourself a level.

Purpose and audience		Text structure
It is sometimes clear who you are writing for and you have used some of the features of a story narrative.	You have written your story as a first-person narrative.	Your story follows a simple structure of a story arc with a beginning, a middle and an end.
It is often clear who you are writing for and you have used many features of a story narrative.	You have written your story as a first-person narrative and mostly in a narrative style.	Your story follows the usual structure of a story arc with a beginning, a middle and an end. It also includes rising tension in the action, description and a resolution.
It is clear who you are writing for and you have used the features of a story narrative.	You have written your story as a first-person narrative all the way through and in a narrative style.	Your story follows the usual structure of a story arc with a beginning, a middle and an end. It also includes rising tension in the action, description and an effective resolution. It includes convincing detail about character and action.

Glossary of key terms

accent: how spoken language sounds in different places (sometimes shown by different spellings – for example, 'Gwan' for 'Go on' in Caribbean English)

adverbial clause: a group of words that tells us more about how or when an action is done, e.g. '*Before I go to bed*, I brush my teeth'

alliteration: the same letter or sound at the start of a group of words (e.g. 'the *l*ovely *l*ark's *l*ilting song')

argument writing: a type of text that argues for a point of view, through considering and dismissing different ideas, before coming to a conclusion

assonance: use of similar or identical vowel sounds in groups of words (e.g. 'the h*oo*ded man in the w*oo*ds')

biased: showing favour towards one side of an argument more than another; showing favour for or against someone or something

characterisation: the way a character is created and developed by a writer

chronological: written and organised in the order in which events happened

comma splice: an error in which a sentence is divided by a comma, when a new sentence, a conjunction or a semicolon is needed (e.g. 'He got angry, the phone didn't work.')

complex sentence: a sentence that contains a supporting idea expressed in a subordinate clause, which adds to the information in the main idea expressed in the main clause

compound sentence: a sentence that contains equally weighted simple sentences joined by connectives

compound word: two words joined together to form a new word

connective: a linking word or phrase used in a sentence (e.g. 'and', 'but', 'or', 'so', 'then', 'because', 'after')

dialect: grammar or vocabulary specific to a place (e.g. 'cobber' is a word meaning 'friend' in Australia)

direct address: the use of the pronoun 'you' in a text to make the reader feel as if the writer is addressing them personally

dual narrators: two narrators who take turns to tell the story from their viewpoint

empathise: to understand the feelings of others

explicit information: information that can be retrieved directly without having to read between the lines

feature article: an article in a newspaper or magazine that deals with a topic in depth

imagery: language intended to conjure up a vivid picture in the reader's mind

implicit: what is shown or suggested in a text (the writer does not provide this information directly but gives the reader clues)

imply: to suggest something, through your choice of words, rather than saying it directly

infer: to work out what someone is implying through their choice of words

informal language: a more personal, chatty way of writing or speaking

metaphor: a type of comparison that describes one thing as if it is something else (e.g. 'Our garden is a jungle')

motive: the reason for behaving in a particular way

narrative perspective: the viewpoint from which a story is told

narrator: the person telling the story or recounting what happened

non-standard English: English that features local or socially different grammar or vocabulary from standard English

noun phrase: a noun with additional information, for example, with an adjective: '*hot* weather'; the noun is called the head word in a noun phrase

onomatopoeia: when a word sounds like the thing it describes (e.g. 'whisper', 'crash')

pace: the speed at which you speak

parenthetical punctuation: pairs of commas, dashes or brackets that create a subordinate to add detail or personal opinion

pathetic fallacy: using a description of the weather to reflect the feelings of a character

preposition: a word that goes before a noun to describe its relationship to another thing or person ('on the table', 'by my bed')

prepositional phrase: a group of words that begins with a preposition and ends with a noun or pronoun ('above the track', 'over the lake')

pronoun: a word used instead of a noun, such as 'he', 'she', 'it', 'they', 'we', 'I', 'you'

rhetorical question: a question that is used to make people think, rather than requiring an answer

rule of three: a useful pattern of three examples, which makes the information or idea expressed memorable

set: the objects and designs that create the idea of a place on a stage

semicolon (;): used to connect two independent clauses (clauses that could each be a sentence on their own)

simile: a comparison between two things that uses the words 'as' or 'like' (e.g. 'Our garden is like a jungle')

simple sentence: a sentence that contains one subject and one verb (e.g. 'The bell rang.')

slang: informal language, often common to a particular group of people (e.g. teens)

stage direction: an instruction within a playscript describing how the text should be performed

standard English: the most widely used form of English which is not specific to a particular place or region

statistics: numbers such as percentages, often used as facts to support a point

subordinating conjunction: a word used to link clauses in a complex sentence (e.g. 'although', 'while', 'when', 'if')

story arc: the full plot of a story – beginning, middle and end

synthesise: bring together ideas from two different sources

topic sentence: a sentence in a paragraph – usually at the beginning – that shows the reader the main subject of the writing

viewpoint: the attitude or feelings a writer or character has towards people or events

voice: the distinctive way a story is told from a character's perspective

Acknowledgements

We are grateful to the following for permission to reproduce copyright material:

An extract on pp.9-10 from *Noah Barleywater Runs Away* by John Boyne, David Fickling Books, copyright © John Boyne, 2010. Reproduced by permission of The Random House Group Limited; Extracts on pp.13, 15 from "Meet Benedict Allen, the explorer rescued by the Daily Mail against his will" by Stephen Moss, *The Guardian*, 28/06/2018, copyright © Guardian News & Media Ltd 2020; An extract on pp.20–21 from *The God of Small Things* by Arundhati Roy, Flamingo, 1998, p.88, copyright © Arundhati Roy 1998. Reproduced by permission of David Godwin Associates Ltd; An extract on p.44 from 'MRI – Magnetic Resonance Imaging' https://www.wsh. nhs.uk/CMS-Documents/Patient-leaflets/Radiology/6148-1-MRI-leaflet-for-children-Mr-Mole.pdf, 26/04/2018, Source: Radiology, Reference No: 6148-2, copyright © West Suffolk NHS Foundation Trust. Reproduced with permission from Alder Hey Children's Hospital, Liverpool; An extract on p.48 'What is a Satellite?' https://www. nasa.gov/audience/forstudents/5-8/features/nasa-knows/what-is-a-satellite-58.html, 12/02/2014. Source: NASA; An extract on p.53 from "Father of the Bicycle and Who Invented It" by Geri Walton, https://www.geriwalton. com/the-bicycle/. Reproduced by kind permission of the author; An extract on p.72 from "How do Google's driverless cars work?" by Victoria Woollaston, https://www.alphr.com/cars/7038/how-do-googles-driverless-cars-work, 04/04/16. Reproduced by kind permission of the author; Extract about Active & Adventure on p.82 from Visit Scotland, www.visitscotland.com, copyright © 2019. Reproduced with permission; An extract on p.86 from "Wingsuit Daredevil Jeb Corliss Completes Another Heart-Stopping 'Flight'" by Meera Dolasia, 30/09/2013, http://www.dogonews.com, copyright © DOGO Media, Inc. Reproduced with permission; An extract about Skydiving & Parachuting on p.88, from Discover Northern Ireland, http://www.discovernorthernireland.com, copyright © 2015. Reproduced with permission; An extract on p.90 from 'Location: Dakar Rally' https://rally. hondaracingcorporation.com/location/dakar-rally/, copyright © Honda Racing Corporation; An extract on p.92 about the British 12 Hour Lawnmower Race, www.blmra.co.uk, British Lawn Mower Racing Association/ BLMRA. Reproduced with permission; An extract on p.101 from "Asia online brochure" by Su-Jit Lin, edited by Kelly Anne Gould, http://www.travimp.com/brochures/, 2018, copyright © Travel Impressions Ltd. Reproduced with permission; Extracts on pp.118–119, 120, 124, 126 from *Follow the Rabbit-Proof Fence* by Doris Pilkington, University of Queensland Press, pp.84–85, copyright © Doris Pilkington and University of Queensland Press, 2002. Reproduced with permission; Extracts on pp.150–151, 152, 168 from *I will marry when I want* by Ngugi wa Thiong'o, published in from *Scenes and Stages*, ed by John O'Connor, Heinemann, 2001, pp.148–152. Reproduced by permission of the author; Extracts on pp.154, 155 from *Running Dream* by Trish Cooke, published in *Six Plays by Black and Asian Women Writers* ed by Kadija George, Aurora Metro Press, pp.190–191. Reproduced by permission of David Higham Associates; The poem on p.172 'Tich Miller' by Wendy Copy from *Making Cocoa for Kingsley Amis* by Wendy Cope, Faber & Faber Ltd, 1986, copyright © Wendy Cope. Reproduced by permission Faber & Faber Ltd and United Agents (www.unitedagents.co.uk) on behalf of Wendy Cope; Poems on pp.178–179, 190 'The Dare' and 'Partners' from *Midnight Forest* by Judith Nicholls, copyright © Judith Nicholls, 1987, published by Faber & Faber. Reproduced by permission of the author; The poem on p.181, 'Only the Moon' by Wong May, translated by E. Thumboo, from *Seven Poets*, Singapore University Press, copyright © NUS Press PTE Ltd; An extract on p.196 from 'Foot and mouth disease', based on a text by Dr Dan Rutherford, GP. Reviewed by Dr Jeni Worden, GP, last updated 31/01/2014. http:// www.netdoctor.co.uk, copyright © Hearst Magazines UK. Reproduced courtesy of Netdoctor; and extracts on p.200–201, 202, 213 from *Out of the Ashes* by Michael Morpurgo, pp.74–76, Macmillan 2002. Reproduced by permission of David Higham Associates.

In some instances we have been unable to trace the owners of copyright material, and we would appreciate any information that would enable us to do so.

The publishers would like to thank the following for permission to reproduce copyright images:
(t = top, b = bottom, c = centre, l = left, r = right)

p7 United Archives GmbH/Alamy Stock Photo, pp8–9 Pajac Slovensky/Shutterstock, pp10–11 Paolo Gallo/ Shutterstock, p13 adrian arbib/Alamy Stock Photo, p15 Album/Alamy Stock Photo, p16 Bellephoto/ Shutterstock, p18 United Archives GmbH/Alamy Stock Photo, p20 P Maxwell Photography/Shutterstock, p23 Kovalev Maxim/Shutterstock, p24 Monkey Business Images/Shutterstock, p27 AF archive/Alamy Stock Photo, p29 sianc/Shutterstock, p30 Mikhail_Kayl/Shutterstock, p32 Ververidis Vasilis/Shutterstock, p33 Karpova/ Shutterstock, p34 Rawpixel.com/Shutterstock, p35 Katvic/Shutterstock, p37 gerritvanrensburg/Shutterstock, p39 Elena Rostunova/Shutterstock, p41 ITAR-TASS News Agency/Alamy Stock Photo, p44 NHS West Suffolk, p45 lapandr Shutterstock, p46 Glasshouse Images/Alamy Stock Photo, p47 Marijana Batinic/Shutterstock, p48 Andrey Armyagov/Shutterstock, p51 MYALA88/Alamy Stock Photo, p53 Denis Doronin/Shutterstock, p54 koya979/Shutterstock, p55 Atstock Productions/Shutterstock, p56 travelwild/Shutterstock, p59 cybrain/ Shutterstock, p60 iurii/Shutterstock, p62 antoniodiaz/Shutterstock, p64 metamorworks/Shutterstock, p65 Sompop Stitvarakom/Shutterstock, p66 Shawn Hempel/Shutterstock, p67 addkm/Shutterstock, p68 Scorpp/ Shutterstock, p70 Brian A Jackson/Shutterstock, p71 Anatoliy Sadovskiy/Shutterstock, p72 metamorworks/ Shutterstock, p74 SiliconValleyStock/Alamy Stock Photo, p77 Ammit Jack/Shutterstock, pp78–79 maxpro/ Shutterstock, pp80–81 Maciej Kopaniecki/Shutterstock, p82 Christian Musat/Shutterstock, p83 dnaveh/ Shutterstock, p85 robertonencini/Shutterstock, p86 Joe Seer/Shutterstock, p87 Teow Cek Chuan/Shutterstock, p88 Germanskydiver/Shutterstock, p89 Germanskydiver/Shutterstock, p90 Christian Vinces/Shutterstock, p92 Rodrigo Garrido/Shutterstock, p94 Christian Kober 1/Alamy Stock Photo, p96 Ersler Dmitry/Shutterstock, p97 Monkey Business Images/Shutterstock, p98 Thongchai S/Shutterstock, p99 Flystock/Shutterstock, p100 sirtravelalot/Shutterstock, p101 Manamana/Shutterstock, pp102–103 gorillaimages/Shutterstock, p104l Chrislofotos/Shutterstock, p104r Dmitry Molchanov/Shutterstock, p105 Santiago Cornejo/Shutterstock, p107 OSTILL is Franck Camhi/Shutterstock, p108 cornfield/Shutterstock, p109 vedrana2701/Shutterstock, p110–111 NOWAK LUKASZ/Shutterstock, p112 Taras Hipp/Shutterstock, p115 GIROMIN STUDIO/Shutterstock, p117 P-fotography/Shutterstock, p119 Photo 12/Alamy Stock Photo, p120 Daisy Daisy/Shutterstock, p123 Tivanova/ Shutterstock, p124 Susan Flashman/Shutterstock, p127 Michael Leslie/Shutterstock, p129 AF archive/Alamy Stock Photo, p130 SpeedKingz/Shutterstock, p133 Monkey Business Images/Shutterstock, p134 The Print Collector/Alamy Stock Photo, p135 Sergey Molchenko/Shutterstock, p138 Motortion Films/Shutterstock, p141 sruilk/Shutterstock, p142 lapandr/Shutterstock, p144 Neal Pritchard Media/Shutterstock, p146 TCD/Prod.DB/ Alamy Stock Photo, p149 SpeedKing /Shutterstock, p150 John Wollwerth/Shutterstock, p153 blickwinkel/ Alamy Stock Photo, p155 Yuliya Yesina/Shutterstock, p159 imageBROKER/Alamy Stock Photo, pp160–161 Photographee.eu/Shutterstock, p162 Lynn Kay/Shutterstock, p166 Jandrie Lombard/Shutterstock, p169 Marcus Stevens/Shutterstock, p171 Vasilyev Alexandr/Shutterstock, p172 redsnapper/Alamy Stock Photo, pp174–175 Pictorial Press Ltd/Alamy Stock Photo, p177 Bachkova Natalia/Shutterstock, p178 Tomasz Kaszuba/ Shutterstock, p181 Przemek Iciak/Shutterstock, p182 Serrgey75/Shutterstock, p183 Bapida Shutterstock, p186 Promotion King/Shutterstock, p188 Erickson Stock/Shutterstock, p190 Marmaduke St. John/Alamy Stock Photo, p192 patat/Shutterstock, p195 Ewelina Wachala/Shutterstock, p197 Volodymyr Burdiak/Shutterstock, p198 DmyTo/Shutterstock, p201 Jan Faukner/Shutterstock, p202 Andrew Roland/Shutterstock, p205 Edgar G Biehle/ Shutterstock, p209 junpiiiiiiiiii/Shutterstock, p211 Ben Carlson/Shutterstock, p213 Smileus/Shutterstock, p216 Pepgooner/Shutterstock